STRATEGIES FOR STILLWATER

The tackle, techniques, and flies for taking trout in lakes and ponds

Dave Hughes

STACKPOLE
BOOKS

Copyright © 1991 by Dave Hughes

Published by
STACKPOLE BOOKS
Cameron and Kelker Streets
P.O. Box 1831
Harrisburg, PA 17105

Printed in the United States of America

10   9   8   7   6   5   4   3   2   1

First edition

Illustrations by Richard Bunse

Library of Congress Cataloging-in-Publication Data

Hughes, Dave.
    Strategies for stillwater/Dave Hughes.
        p.   cm.
    Includes bibliographical references and index.
    ISBN 0-8117-1916-2
    1. Trout fishing. 2. Fly fishing. 3. Lake fauna. 4. Pond fauna.
I. Title.
SH687.H762   1991
799.1'755 – dc20   91-8427
                                                                        CIP

*To my brother Barney,
who shared much of that
earliest exploratory fishing.*

Contents

Introduction   vii

Part I: Reading Stillwaters

Chapter 1: The Needs of Trout   2

Chapter 2: Structure of a Stillwater   20

Chapter 3: Plant Life in Lakes   33

Part II: Strategies for Stillwaters

Chapter 4: Gearing Up for Ponds and Lakes   44

Chapter 5: Aquatic Transportation   66

Chapter 6: The Three Major Variables   81

Chapter 7: The Dry Fly and Reluctant Trout   89

Chapter 8: The Dry Fly and Rising Trout   98

Chapter 9: Nymph Strategies   114

Chapter 10: Wet Fly Strategies   133

Chapter 11: Streamer Strategies   140

Chapter 12: Trolling and Wind-drifting   153
Chapter 13: Sight Fishing   162

Part III: Lake Food Forms and Their Imitations

Chapter 14: When Trout Are Active   172
Chapter 15: Mayflies   175
Chapter 16: Caddisflies   191
Chapter 17: Midges   200
Chapter 18: Dragonflies and Damselflies   208
Chapter 19: Alderflies   218
Chapter 20: Water Boatmen and Back Swimmers   224
Chapter 21: Scuds and Other Crustaceans   230
Chapter 22: Leeches   237

Conclusion: Let Lakes Come to You   242
Bibliography   243
Index   245

Introduction

It was a big lake, half a mile across and twice that long. Rumor reported that it contained big trout. I fished it according to what I had heard about its trout and could see of its size, wading out as deep as possible and using stout gear to propel big streamers as far as I could toss them. I retrieved fast, held on for the big hit, and listened to the angry outbursts of a hundred coots arguing about mating territories in the reed beds along the shoreline.

Jim Schollmeyer listened to a different tune, however, and he approached the lake in a different way.

"Aren't those midges?" he'd cocked his head and asked when we'd first waded in. I had cocked my head, too, and had listened to a whine that sounded just like a high-tension electric line overhead. But it wasn't powerlines making that noise – it was a vast swarm of midges swirling in the sun, setting up the sound of so many tiny wingbeats that a constant whine rose and fell with the wind.

Jim waded out just knee-deep, while I pushed up a bow wave far out beyond him. He rigged a light rod and tried a succession of small midge nymphs in the shallows, while I patiently cast my streamer toward the depths and listened to the quarreling coots.

Neither of us got a nibble at first. After a while we had drifted a hundred yards apart. I heard a shout and turned to see Jim still standing in knee-deep water but now leaning back against a bent rod, playing a trout that galumphed around in the inches-deep water next to the sagebrush shore. The trout must have dashed in there in panic. It was almost stranded. It was so big that its back came half out of the water as it wallowed around.

Jim subdued the fish and released it, and I dismissed it as a fluke. All the other trout were still out in big water where they belonged, and they still wanted my big fly. I turned my back to Jim and continued casting and retrieving.

In minutes I heard a second shout. Jim had hooked another trout in the shallows. I reeled up and dashed over to the scene of all the action. Even if it was an accident, I wanted to find out why it had happened to Jim and not to me. I arrived about the time he was ready to release the fish. It was a cutthroat, nearly 20 inches long. I admired the fish with him, then glanced at the fly in its lip, which was what I was truly there for. It was so small that it looked silly perched in that big lip.

Jim returned to his fishing. I returned to mine, too. But I stayed near, where I could keep an eye on Jim while I fished. Strangely, when he began casting again, he turned his back to the lake and made his casts almost to the shoreline. His retrieve was a hand-twist that crept the fly through the shallows.

I didn't believe it was a fly and a method that would work consistently on such big water, taking fish so large that they obviously would want fuel that came in bigger bites. But suddenly a V-wake formed and pointed at Jim's fly. The water welled up, and then Jim was hollering and leaning against a bent rod again.

I always hate asking for advice because I dislike lectures. But Jim always makes it sound like he stumbles on to what works by accident, which I would believe if he didn't stumble on to what works so often. At least he doesn't lecture.

"They're taking a size sixteen Zug Bug," Jim told me when I asked him what he was using. "But I don't know why."

He knew why. They were taking it because it resembled the pupal stage of the insect that had become all of those midges up in the air. The water was opaque, and he couldn't see the trout or what they were eating. He didn't have an insect net, so he couldn't collect the insects. He didn't want to kill a fish, so he couldn't confirm his hunch. But he worked through a litany of likely nymphs until he found one that the trout approved. Then he called it an accident, which it wasn't.

Neither was it an accident that he fished the fly in the shallows behind him rather than the deep water in front of him. An occasional swirl happened in there, almost invisible. It was a trout turning to take something subsurface. Each slight swirl was the indicator of an "iceberg," the proof of a pod of trout cruising in the shallows.

A fly cast there and retrieved slowly was sure to be seen by a trout or two. The slow retrieve was no idle matter, either. Jim keyed it to what he knew about the behavior of immature midges. They don't frisk around; they can hardly swim.

I was overeager. I was in a hurry to lean back against one of those big fish that Jim had been landing. So I rigged right, with the same #16 Zug Bug, and cast it in the right direction, in toward shore. But I brought the fly back with jerky strips, trying to coax the fish into sharing my eagerness. They didn't.

Jim watched my retrieve. "Slow down, dammit!" he recommended.

I did. Soon an arrow pointed at my fly, and the water welled up around it. Then, while I played the trout, inexplicably as it always happens when fly-fishing for trout, I got the feeling that I'd figured it all out for myself.

Lakes are not entirely different from streams, although things are not always quite so clearly defined in stillwaters as they are when the water is moving. But even when you're fishing a big lake for big fish, as Jim and I were doing, you'll do best when you tie your hopes into some sort of structure that indicates potential holding water or some sort of signal that trout are around and willing to feed. Then tie your fly selection to some sort of food form that interests the trout.

Then it can become productive and fun.

This is the companion book to my series on strategies for streams, which includes *Handbook of Hatches, Reading the Water,*

Tackle and Technique, and *Tactics for Trout.* Those books cover fly-fishing for trout in moving waters: how to recognize the hatches and match them, how to find the trout and fool them, how to select tackle and cast well with it, and how to put all of those factors together into a wide-ranging set of tactics that take trout.

This book, *Strategies for Stillwater,* covers the same set of subjects for lakes and ponds: how to recognize and match lake food forms, how to find trout beneath the sometimes blank slate of a lake's surface, how to gear up to fish lakes correctly, and how to put all the other factors together into proper fly selection and a set of strategies to take stillwater trout.

I hope it helps to make stillwater trout fishing productive and fun for you.

Part I
Reading Stillwaters

1

The Needs of Trout

Trout are found in stillwaters, as they are in streams, in accordance with the way the water meets their basic needs. Trout in lakes and ponds have four essential requirements. The first, which they often neglect in their eager search for food, is protection from predators. The second, which they are not allowed to forget, is an acceptable temperature and oxygen regime. The third is an annual need for suitable spawning areas. The fourth and final one, the one that propels them most often into danger from anglers, is food.

The requirement for shelter from exhausting currents, elemental in running water, is not present in stillwater. That need to dodge brisk flows, when combined with the need to be where they can find food drifting on a current, makes reading trout water in streams relatively easy compared to reading stillwaters. Lack of the primary need to fight currents is the missing link that makes reading stillwaters more difficult. But it's far from impossible; it's often just as easy as reading a stream once you learn how a lake meets the needs of a trout.

To hook a trout in a stillwater, you have to remember that you are a
predator, and you must get past the trout's defenses. *Jim Schollmeyer*

PROTECTION FROM PREDATORS

This requirement gets at least partially neglected when trout rise
up high in the water to feed on a hatch of insects. We've all seen
the sudden swoop and splash of an osprey, and we've all seen one
slowly lifting off while adjusting a careless trout into an aero-
dynamic position in its talons. But it's not all so simple that you
can neglect it. When trout rise up high to feed in apparent reck-
lessness, they're more vulnerable to predation, and therefore more
wary, just as they are when feeding on a spring creek flat. Wave
your line over their heads while they cruise the breathless surface
of a stillwater and you'll get an abrupt report about that.

It might seem that the need for protection from predators
couldn't mean much when it comes to reading water and finding
fish in lakes. But it becomes very important once you recall that
you're the predator. You have to get past a trout's defenses before
you can coax it to the fly and feel its weight dangling pleasantly in
your landing net.

Some of the defenses that protect trout are natural features of lakes: weed beds, the darkness of a sudden drop-off in depth, tangles of logs and limbs, jumbles of boulders. These, of course, are called cover. You've got to scout them out and explore them with flies.

Other defenses are features of the time of day or what weather the day brings: the secure darkness of night, the slight dimness of cloud shadow, the surface disruption of wind-riffling. All of these help to conceal trout from their natural predators. They also make trout easier for the angler to approach.

The most important defenses of a trout are its senses: sight, hearing, the tactile sense of the lateral line, and the linked senses of smell, taste, and texture.

Sight is the trout's most important defense. This is evidenced by the outsized optical lobes in the trout brain. The parts of the brain that serve the other senses are much smaller. The cerebral regions, so large in the head of the average fly fisherman, are embarrassingly small in his quarry.

Trout can see underwater about as far as you can see into it, or could see through it if you poked your head under it and gazed around. Underwater vision is affected by the intensity of light and the presence of turbidity. In perfect conditions a trout might be able to see thirty to fifty feet or more, perceiving you as a predator at that range if your moves are threatening. If your moves are not threatening, you can approach much closer. If you don't move at all, trout will come right to you. I've had trout in lakes turn aside to avoid bumping into my wader-clad legs when I held perfectly still.

When the water is cloudy with a plankton bloom or suspended silt, vision is reduced to two to five feet or so. Your own movements are obviously not such a problem then.

An interesting implication stemming from the clarity of water was pointed out by Ernest Schwiebert in his brilliant book *Trout:* In cloudy water you should place your casts a yard or so apart, while in clear water, where trout can easily see a fly at ten feet or so, it's wiser to space them farther apart, allowing you to explore more water.

For a trout, sight above the water is restricted to a circular window straight overhead. This circle goes with them wherever they swim; it grows narrower as they approach the surface,

The trout sees the world above water through a circular window that is distorted around the edges and clearer as objects move toward the center of it.

broader as they move down in the water column. Objects straight overhead are clear because the light rays that represent them enter the water without bending. Objects at the periphery of the circle are distorted and compacted because light rays that represent them are bent and compressed by the angle of refraction.

As an angler you are almost always out toward the periphery of a trout's window of vision. Beyond forty feet you're far enough toward the edge of it to be small and distorted. But even out there a fast move will alarm trout if they're feeding or cruising in clear and unruffled water.

As you move closer than forty feet, you begin to loom higher and higher over the trout. A trout visible at twenty feet will almost always bolt if you cast with a high rod while it's heading your way. Whatever you can do to lower your profile will increase your odds. That is why a float tuber can fish right among a pod of trout while a boat angler must get off to the edge of the pod and cast toward it.

Sounds made underwater travel very well through that medium, and trout have excellent internal ears. Any banging in a boat, or thudding as you walk along an undercut shore, will be delivered to them as a warning. Just the other day my dad and I saw an excellent example of the reaction of trout to noise. We rowed our prams around a tree-rimmed lake. A few alderflies were out in the sunshine, and a few rainbow trout anxiously thumped our imitations.

Dad's boat was wood, a material that is inherently quiet. My boat was a small fiberglass drift boat, not naturally quiet but easy to quell with some caution. A couple of folks arrived later, launched an aluminum boat, and went clanking after the trout. Their boat was inherently noisy, and they had no concept that sound was something bad. The noise they made was enough to alarm me, and I'm not a trout.

The worst of it was that Dad and I were hooking enough trout to make these poor folks jealous. Every time one of us got a fish up and dancing, they'd bang over toward us to get nearer to what they perceived as the scene of success. We were forced to row away from them to get back into fish that weren't frightened. Then we'd hook another, and they'd row after us again. It almost became a chase.

Sounds generated in air – above the water and not made in contact with it – do not penetrate from air into water. You can crash your oars together like cymbals in the air, and trout will never notice. You can shout and whoop and holler, and they'll never know it's happening. But thump the boat lightly and they'll be displeased.

The tactile sense of the lateral line gives trout a feel for low-range vibrations. In a way it is an extension of the sense of sound: Trout can hear a sharp rap on your boat, but they also can sense the vibrations of a dull thud that you thought you got away with. It's a separate sense unique to fish. We don't possess it, although at one time we might have. It means that you have to be even more careful about movement in your boat or of footfalls along the shoreline.

The trout's sense of smell is relatively acute, and this has many implications. There are many reasons not to tinkle over the side of your boat – sanitation and the chance of a swim among them – but you're also going to send trout messages over quite a circle around the boat.

The smell of sunscreen is frightening to fish. Although it's necessary gear, keep it off your fingers, your flies, and your leader. It can reduce your odds to nearly zero, and you'll always blame it on something else.

Mosquito repellent can be just as bad. Again, use it, but keep it off your terminal gear. You can dress against mosquitoes – I consider the canvas shirt one of the greatest inventions in fly-fishing – but it's hard to fish on a hot day while wearing gloves.

I've known anglers who braved mosquitoes rather than risk scaring fish. I gathered up with Ron Van Fleet and Rick Newton, members of the notorious Rainland Flycasters out of my home town, Astoria, Oregon, one evening during a raid on a Washington lake. Bugs were out and so fierce that I'd lathered up against them. Fishing was slow for me. Ron swished his hat through the air, did a little dance, and swore at the mosquitoes attacking him.

"I have some mosquito repellent here in my vest," I offered.

"No thanks," Ron said. "I'd rather catch fish."

Taste is something you can't do much about. A fly is bound to taste bad no matter what materials you use to tie it. But the sense for texture is something else. Flies tied of soft and natural materials such as fur or chenille are likely to be held a second or so longer than flies tied with hard plastic parts. This can mean the difference between a take you detect and a take you don't even know happened.

I've overlooked flight as a trout defense. It's the one you'll see most often when you've failed to get past their other senses. When you witness flight, you're being scolded.

OXYGEN AND TEMPERATURE

Oxygen and water temperature are interrelated needs because temperature affects the amount of oxygen entrained in water, and also because trout require more oxygen when water temperatures rise. Thus, when they seek a comfort zone, it is a search for a depth at which both needs are met in one place, in some sort of compromise.

Most of the time all of the water throughout a lake or pond satisfies both needs. When that is true, oxygen and temperature do not limit trout movements and do not help you locate them. Only in certain extremes do the twin needs come to the forefront and tell you where trout might be found.

When lakes stratify in summer, usually in late June through early September, the midwater thermocline contains little oxygen because it doesn't circulate, thus becoming stagnant. Deeper water, beneath the thermocline, although colder, also holds too little oxygen to support trout. They avoid both areas.

The entire layer of water above the thermocline is constantly mixed by wind and, therefore, is constantly replenished with atmospheric oxygen and with oxygen generated from plant photo-synthesis. During normal times, when water temperatures are in the comfort range for trout, 70 degrees or below, trout can be found in all of the water above the thermocline but rarely in it or below it. If temperatures rise toward discomfort levels above the thermocline, trout drop down toward the cool thermocline itself but stay far enough above it to remain in oxygenated water.

In a stratified lake, trout hold only in the wind-mixed and therefore oxygenated water above the thermocline.

The thermocline will be about fifteen to twenty feet down in most trout lakes of small to medium size and average water clarity. In large lakes, especially with clear water, the thermocline drops to thirty or forty feet, perhaps even deeper. In shallow lakes and ponds, fifteen feet or less, the water seldom stratifies.

You can see how this knowledge about temperature and oxy-gen helps you locate trout. More to the point, it helps you elimi-nate water where you won't find trout when a lake is stratified. In a lake with no depths greater than about fifteen feet, they might be anywhere because there is no stratification. In an average lake with depths down to fifty or sixty feet, the trout will be located in the upper twenty feet, above the thermocline. In large and deep lakes trout will be in the upper thirty to forty feet. This does not pinpoint them by any means, but it does eliminate a lot of water that you would waste time fishing.

Lake trout, or mackinaw, seem to break all these rules. They descend to great depths during the summer. But they are restricted to lakes that either do not stratify, so that oxygen is delivered by mixing far into the cold depths, or to lakes that are so large and clear that they stratify at seventy-five feet down to 150 feet.

During hot spells, when water temperatures above the thermocline soar over 70 degrees, trout are forced to seek a comfortable compromise level, where oxygen is still available but the temperature is more acceptable. During these periods the oxygen/temperature need can help you pinpoint the depth at which trout hold. They drop down to hold just above the thermocline, where they find oxygen still abundant but the water cooled by proximity to the colder thermocline.

In an average lake, with its thermocline at fifteen to twenty feet, you can expect to find trout just above that level, at twelve to eighteen feet during long hot spells. In a large lake, with its thermocline at thirty to forty feet, trout again will be just above it, at twenty-five to thirty-five feet.

When the weather is hot, it will pay you to dangle a thermometer over the side to determine the depth at which there's a sudden drop in temperature. That marks the thermocline. Then choose a sinking-line rate and a speed of retrieve that lets you fish just above that depth.

It's not as simple in lakes too shallow to stratify. But oxygen and temperature can still help you find trout. Shallow lakes tend to be eutrophic: nutrient rich and somewhat cloudy. In turbid water, sunlight and the heat it delivers are absorbed faster than in clear water. The surface layers heat up more quickly, and temperatures drop off as you go down, especially if wind-mixing is minimal during a spell of weather that is both hot and breathless. Theoretically, trout would go right to the bottom. However, there's another factor to consider.

Nutrient-rich lakes often have a rich layer of organic detritus along the bottom: decaying plant and animal life that forms a soft ooze. This layer of ooze holds little oxygen because most of it is used up by the process of decay. As a consequence, the bottom itself won't hold any fish at all in an extremely rich lake because of the lack of oxygen. When exploring shallow but rich lakes or ponds for trout that have moved away from the surface due to high water temperatures, fish deep but avoid fishing the bottom. Keep your fly two to four feet above it and you will have it in the zone that is coolest yet still has lots of oxygen. This narrows your search area down considerably.

Shallow waters that are clear and have clean bottoms do not have a layer of decaying ooze. The depths are not depleted of oxygen. In these kinds of lakes the bottom is the most likely place to find trout when the weather is hot.

Trout will gather around any cool spring when the weather gets hot. When things are slow and a lake seems heat-bound, it is often worth the time it takes to drop a thermometer down and sample water temperatures at various points in a lake. If you come up with an area that is abruptly cooler than the areas around it, concentrate your fishing there.

Any inflow that delivers cool water will gather trout around it during a hot spell. There are so many other reasons to fish at the mouth of a stream that they should never be overlooked, even when the weather is not so hot that oxygen and temperature become important factors in locating trout.

During normal weather, when water temperatures are in the comfortable range and wind-mixing keeps oxygen circulating throughout the layers above any thermocline, temperature and oxygen are not limiting factors. They don't do much to help you locate trout. You have to look at the other needs.

SPAWNING

Brown, rainbow, and cutthroat trout all require moving water to spawn successfully. To contain self-sustaining populations of these species, a lake must have feeder streams. In the absence of spawning tributaries these trout will attempt to deposit and fertilize their eggs in gravel shallows and along wave-washed shorelines, but they won't cause much propagation.

Brook trout are able to spawn and populate a lake or pond in the absence of feeder streams. They cast their eggs over gravel beds or rocks and boulders, in water shallow enough to enjoy some sun. Because of this fine ability, brookies are the only species likely to overpopulate a stillwater, sometimes taxing food supplies to the point that the fish become stunted. This is especially true in high-mountain lakes that get little fishing pressure and also have a short growing season. Such waters are often full of pestery little

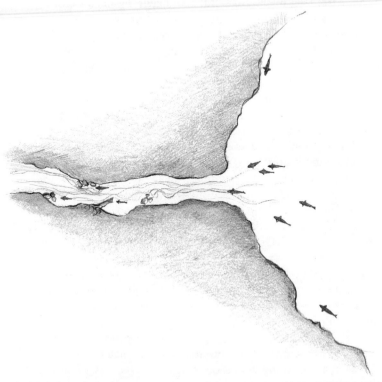

Trout gather around creek mouths in preparation for their spawning run.

brookies that fit several in a frying pan and taste great fried in butter. There's no reason not to eat them.

Rainbows and cutts are spring spawners, gathering at the deltas of feeders in April and May, or in the weeks just after ice-out. I once damaged my reputation by hooking thirty Lahontan cutthroat on the same number of casts on a May trip to a desert lake. The trout were gathered around a meager and muddy inflow. One of the casts failed to hook a trout, but on another I hooked one and lost it and another picked up the fly before I had time to lift it up and cast again, so I kept my record intact.

Brookies also spawn in spring, gathering around the same feeder streams, or over shoreline shallows in the absence of them. Such gatherings of any species are rarely so dramatic that you can hook a trout on every cast. But the spawning urge does tend to deliver trout to feeder streams in early spring, and it's the first place to look for them at that time of year.

Brown trout spawn in fall, collecting for runs into tributaries in late September and October. When such gathering is going on, it condenses the fish, and your chance for a trophy is correspondingly high. At that time of year, in the absence of other clues such as visibly rising or feeding fish, concentrate your fishing around entering streams, or at least give them a patient try.

Access to adequate spawning water can regulate the population of rainbow, cutthroat, or brown trout in a lake or pond. Some stillwaters have lots of spawning mileage entering them, and although the individual trout are small to average in size, their populations tend to be high. Others have little spawning access. In natural conditions, without stocking, these waters tend to have small populations of trout that often grow very large.

Many lakes have no spawning tributaries at all. Without planted trout they would be barren of fish. They can be stocked on a repetitive cycle with any species, although a single stocking of brook trout often results in a long-term population without any further effort.

I have two favorite lakes, almost side by side, that illustrate the difference in spawning potential. One is small and has a small, clean stream running in and out of it. This lake has a fine population of wild cutthroat that run 7 to 10 inches long. It isn't fished much, and I have no hesitation about hiking to it with a frying pan in my pack.

The neighboring lake is larger, but it is spring fed with no inlet or outlet. It has no natural spawning and is stocked sporadically with rainbow trout. This lake has lots of aquatic insects and a natural abundance of crayfish. It doesn't take long for the stockers to catch on to the hatches, and they can be maddeningly selective once they do. After that it doesn't take long for them to get enough growth to start feeding on the crayfish. In the fall they take a sudden leap in size; their heads and tails recede to miniatures at opposite ends of bulbous bodies.

Because every trout killed here early in the season, just after stocking, reduces the number that might be caught later when they've turned into fish with a shape you could punt, I prefer to release them, and I encourage my friends to do the same, even though they're plants. Otherwise the trout population dwindles quickly through the summer, and by fall there are not enough left to make fishing worthwhile.

It's a strange reversal: I don't mind eating the wild fish because they are abundant and have a limit on their potential for size, but I hate to kill the planters because they get going on those crayfish and keep right on growing. A holdover that makes it through the winter will be big enough to growl when it takes a fly the next spring.

FOOD: THE OVERRIDING FACTOR

At most of the times of year that we fish stillwaters for trout and find it a pleasant thing to do, food is what moves the fish into the places where we find them. It is the key that helps to locate trout. That is one of the reasons a book about fishing for trout in still-waters is in large part a study of the foods that trout eat. There is another obvious reason: Flies that resemble those foods are most apt to fool the fish.

The activity of a specific food form, such as this *Callibaetis* mayfly nymph, is often the key to finding and catching trout in stillwaters.

Food is not delivered to trout in stillwaters the same way it is in streams. Trout must seek it out. As a consequence, it is the main motivation for trout movement during spring, summer, and fall. A particular kind of trout food usually has a preference for a certain kind of habitat. When that food becomes most active, say before and during a hatch, then it is also most available, and trout move into the area where the hatch is happening.

As the activity of that food dwindles, another food form might pick up importance in a different kind of habitat. Trout respond by changing addresses, and you'll suddenly find them near shore intercepting a damselfly migration rather than suspended over a weed bed picking off ascending mayfly nymphs.

Part 3 of this book, Lake Food Forms and Their Imitations, deals in detail with the various food forms, their habitat preferences, and how trout respond to their movements. It would be unproductive to go into the various foods here except to say that response to them, especially aquatic insects and crustaceans, is the most important thing to understand when trying to locate trout in stillwaters.

Some food forms are rather rare, existing in scattered populations and seemingly unimportant. But when one stage of one food becomes dominant, even for a short period, and is easy for trout to capture, it is suddenly very important. Trout will be found in the kind of habitat where that form is active, feeding at the level where it moves, looking for something that looks like it and swims, crawls, or creeps as it does.

TROUT MOVEMENTS

I like to think in terms of two kinds of trout movements. First are the major movements that place most trout in specific areas of a lake at certain times of the season, in response to temperature cycles or hatch cycles. Second are the internal movements within these larger areas as the trout cruise in response to changes in light or temperature during the day, or in response to a hatch as it happens.

In streams, 90 percent of the trout are said to reside in 10 percent of the water. I doubt that the percentage is quite that dramatic in moving water, but it might be nearly that dramatic in lakes. Trout in moving water are territorial, but the instinct diminishes as current speed slows. Fish on a flat or in a slow pool often travel in schools. Lakes have subtle currents, but nothing so strong that it would cause any sort of territoriality.

Trout in lakes typically travel in schools, and finding one fish is good evidence that others are around. That is why understanding the types of movement is important.

Major Movements

I've already mentioned two types of major movements: gathering for spawning runs and the movement toward the thermocline during hot spells. Those are specific situations. The first is relatively easy to plumb, since trout will be shallow and holding at limited locations: the mouths of feeder streams or, in the case of brookies, over gravel shallows.

The second movement is not as easy to follow. When trout move down to the thermocline, they're difficult to find even if you know what's happening. The use of electronics – depth finders and fish locators – makes it easier. But electronics are a way of complicating fly-fishing that I haven't accepted yet in my own fishing. Short of such gadgetry, you have to use line types that get your fly to the depths you want to fish, then patiently explore with it.

The most common major trout movements are in response to increased activity and availability of some sort of food form. It's usually an insect: a hatch of mayflies, caddis, or midges, a migration of damselflies, or a fall of terrestrials. Lack of any insect activity, following a peak of it, might prompt a movement back toward waters that consistently hold food forms that don't have hatch periods. For example, after a hatch in the shallows ends, trout might move back over deep weed beds that are loaded with scuds.

Most major trout movements in spring are from deep water into shallows, which vary from a foot deep in turbid water down to fifteen or twenty feet in water clear enough to have vegetation growth at those depths. In essence, in the spring you should be thinking about the limits of light penetration. Weed growth requires sunlight. Insects require weed growth or other kinds of forage associated with photosynthesis.

Aquatic insects need vegetation growth; trout need aquatic insects. In spring, when trout are active, think in terms of the limits of light and fish where the sun causes vegetation to grow.

In midsummer insect activity in the shallows usually slows down following the major hatches of spring. Trout stick to the shallows as long as temperatures are comfortable because there's more food there. But if the temperature rises, trout will look for cool springs or inlet streams, or they will move out and drop toward the thermocline. Keep in mind, however, that this last movement only occurs in waters that stratify, and in which the surface layer gets uncomfortably warm, above 70 to 75 degrees. Even then insect activity will usually prompt fish into following and feeding.

On large lakes, during terrestrial time, you'll often notice a major trout movement into a certain confined area of the lake, usually toward the side from which the wind blows. It is surprising how often such a movement is in response to a fall of beetles, lofted out of the high trees. It's also surprising how difficult it is to spot insects so tiny that they arrive on the wind. On ponds and small lakes a terrestrial fall might generate feeding over the entire surface area.

In autumn the major movements are usually out of the depths and back into the shallows, following a resurgence of insect activity. But this movement is also in response to cooling waters. Fall movements are often sporadic, fitful, and hard to understand. Part of this is due to inconsistent hatches. In spring insect activity causes trout to reveal themselves by their rises. This happens less often in fall. Trout respond whenever insects are available on the surface or under it. But on many lakes hatches are sporadic, and trout rise the same way: one here, another a few minutes later a hundred yards away, then a third one halfway down the shoreline toward where you were ten minutes ago, before you started chasing the one that rose last.

Trout are difficult to pattern when they rise at what seems like random. But it's an indication that they are cruising. If you can define the area in which they cruise, then you've outlined the limits of their major movement. After that you just have to be patient, keeping your fly working within the area, hoping to intercept the flight path of a single fish, or even a school.

To simplify major movements in spring and fall, think of weed growth and the limits of light. That usually means fishing in association with the shoreline or weed beds. In summer trout will stay in the same type of water until temperatures drive them down toward the thermocline or toward cold springs.

Major movements in winter are usually away from shore and toward deeper water, where trout get cryptic. But any time the weather and water are warm enough, trout will be found active and feeding right where they were in spring and fall – in association with photosynthetic growth.

Internal Movements

Within the area of a major movement trout cruise in search of food, or in search of comfort when food isn't active. This might mean a move closer to shore in response to a hatch, then a move offshore after it's over. A sudden change in weather, either hotter or colder, might push fish toward the deepest water in the area.

As an example of internal movement, I was just on a windswept lake in central Washington for a few days. The major movement was easy to figure out. All of the random trout I caught while kicking my tube and trolling or casting were within a couple of hundred feet of the shoreline, and almost always over sparse beds of rooted plants. When the wind slacked off, usually at morning and evening, mayfly spinners came out of the sagebrush and

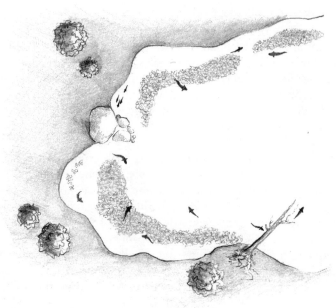

Understanding major movements that put trout in a certain area of a lake, and also internal movements that propel them around the major area, will help you find and catch them.

danced over the lake, landing to deposit their eggs. Trout responded by rising visibly to feed on them in the same area.

Whenever the wind howled, mayflies stayed off the water, visible rises ceased, and I was forced back to trolling or casting in order to find the fish. They remained in the larger area near shore, still cruising along it in an internal movement. But I intercepted them only occasionally. It was impossible to keep touch with a school.

Think what would have happened if I'd just gone out and flailed around on the lake at random, without staying where the major movement put most of the trout most of the time. I'd have only taken trout when my path took me through the area of major movement, and within that across the path of a cruising single trout or school. The odds would have been greatly against me, and would have reduced the number of times my rod took that sudden and satisfying bend.

One important way to plumb internal movements is to see the whole day. If you're going to be on a lake for more than a day, arrange your fishing time so you're on the water from dawn to dusk, although I'm not suggesting that you do it on the same day. That might make too long a day. Get up at dawn one day and fish through early afternoon before quitting. Sleep late the next day, go out at midmorning, and stay on the water until dark. If there is a period of insect activity, and the trout respond by making the exciting internal movement called a feeding spree, you will be sure to know about it. For the rest of the trip you'll be able to enjoy it.

I wouldn't emphasize this quite so strongly if I hadn't once enjoyed a heavy dawn hatch by myself, for several days, on a lake that had an entire fly-fishing club camped on it. I had my best fishing over a dawn hatch of caddis while the club slept. I spent my time in camp while they were out flailing the water unproductively at midmorning, casting over trout that were busy patting their bellies and burping.

One of the most interesting internal movements is the sometimes circular or elliptical path of a feeding school. You can position yourself ahead of them and intercept them each time through, hopefully hooking a fish at each pass, then waiting patiently while they swing around again.

Another form of internal movement is the linear path of a school cruising along a shoreline in their major feeding area. Usually they'll reach a certain point, then disappear, to reappear after a while right back where they started. If they're feeding visibly, you'll see the rises approaching you. If they're feeding underwater and you're in a line of anglers, you'll see rods down the line begin to dip, then the dipping of rods moving closer to you. Get ready.

One of the most frustrating internal movements is the continual drift of a pod of feeding fish away from your boat, float tube, or wading waves. You keep pressing after them, or at least I do, and they keep moving away. The thing to do is back off, quit making waves, and wait for them to move back into casting range. They'll do it. Then you'll catch them.

2

Structure of a Stillwater

Where you find trout in a lake or pond – and the size and shape of the trout that you find – depends on the structure of the stillwater. This structure has three components: physical, thermal, and chemical. They are interrelated, difficult to untangle from each other. But you should try, since each component gives some direction to the movements of trout in a lake.

PHYSICAL STRUCTURE OF A STILLWATER

Lakes cover 1.8 percent of the earth's surface and they come in three kinds. *Drainage lakes* have inlet and outlet streams. They are complete ecosystems, come in all sizes, and normally boast native populations of fish, including trout if temperatures and other characteristics are right for them. If the stream systems that enter and exit a drainage lake hold trout, it is likely that the lake will hold them as well.

Seepage lakes arise from springs and have no tributaries or outflows. They are restricted ecosystems and might hold fish of the kind that can be transported in the egg stage by sticking to the legs of shorebirds. These include bluegills and bullheads, but not trout. Seepage lakes sat by the thousands in our mountain regions providing no trout fishing until trout were brought to them. They have to be planted before they provide trout fishing.

Reservoirs are made by man and have character flaws that are unique and not often beneficial. The constant raising and lowering of reservoir water makes it impossible for a rich shoreline flora to get established. A lake without relatively stable shallows cannot grow weed beds. That's why reservoirs are not as productive as natural lakes.

Natural lakes are formed by the same forces that shape the land around them. Many arise from the tectonic movements that make mountains, creating folds or crevices in the surface that trap and hold water. Other lakes, especially in the desert West, are the remnants of once vast seas and inland lakes.

Glacial meanderings left millions of lakes in the wake of the retreating ice. Some were scoured out of old streambeds; they are long and narrow. Others formed when giant deposits of ice, surrounded by the transported rock and soil of moraines, slowly melted, leaving a lake in the hollow spot. Some of these moraine lakes are very deep and have sharply sloped edges.

Many lakes were formed by earthquakes and consequent landslides that blocked the flow of a river or stream. I've just recently discovered a small pond not far from my home. It didn't take much exploring around its outlet to determine that not long ago in geologic terms a rock slide blocked the creek that flows into and out of the pond. The natural dam is just about worn through now; what was once a fair-sized lake is nothing but a large meadow with a two-acre pond braced against the dam at one end. But it still offers excellent fishing.

Oxbow lakes are formed in courses abandoned by rivers. Since rivers meander and form oxbows in their more dignified lower reaches, these lakes are usually out in the lowlands, shallow and subject to high heat in summer, home for warm-water fish more often than trout.

Seepage lakes often form in mountain basins, gathering water that runs underground rather than over the surface. These lakes are often deep, bedrock-bottomed, blue, and beautiful, although their very beauty is a sign of relative sterility. They often harbor populations of eager little trout that are hungry for flies. But some seepage lakes are rich, especially those that form in soft soils that contain lots of the vital nutrients for plant and animal life. These can be enormously productive, although they've usually got to be stocked with trout on some sort of cycle because the lack of feeder streams also means a lack of spawning grounds.

Physical Factors in Lake Productivity

The altitude of a lake or pond has a vital influence on its trout population. High-altitude lakes, above eight or nine thousand feet, have a short season that is free of ice. This does not affect survival of fish unless the lake is subject to winterkill, which many of them are. But it does affect the growth of trout. High-mountain lakes usually have clean water with few nutrients. This is combined with the limited time during which trout can roam with metabolic abandon. High lakes are known for an abundance of small trout.

Lowland lakes, from sea level up to one or two thousand feet in elevation, are just the opposite. Because their surrounding topographies are typically ancient and worn flat, these waters tend to be shallow, struck by the sun, and very rich. They can be great trout fisheries if they don't become too hot and turn into warm-water fisheries. The chance for a trout to grow large in such waters is excellent.

Lakes in the intermediate elevation zones, three to six thousand feet, often combine the features that we think of as making up a trout lake. They have cool water that is shallow, sunstruck, and vegetated around the edges. They are productive in spring and fall, and deep enough to stratify in midsummer. Most are protected from overheating in the hot months and winterkill in the cold months by their depth.

Latitude is an obvious factor in the productivity of a lake. Most of those in the southern zones exceed the temperature limits of trout – the high 70s or low 80s – unless they are at high elevation. Lakes in the far northern latitudes freeze over and winter-kill unless they have lots of depth, in which case they are excellent for lake trout, which thrive on a diet of baitfish and do well in the open-water depths of big lakes.

The geography surrounding a stillwater, such as this alpine golden trout lake in the High Sierra, will tell you a lot about its nature, and its fishing.

Most trout species have adapted to the range of water temperatures found in the temperate latitudes, however, and that's where trout do best in stillwaters.

The size of a stillwater has a lot to do with its productivity. This is largely related to the limits of light penetration. The bottom of a pond is nearly all lit by the sun and productive. A small lake has more shoreline than it does central depths, and shoreline and shallows are most productive. A large lake has less shoreline in relation to its depths, and unless it has extensive shallows it will not be as productive as a smaller lake, although it might produce bigger trout. That is why ponds sometimes teem with trout, small-to-medium lakes have good populations of fish that are easy to track down, while large lakes have scattered fish that are easy to find at certain times of the year but very difficult to locate at others.

The terrain surrounding a lake often predicts the nature of the lake bed. In the tilted geography of the high mountains, lakes often drop straight off into depths. Such lakes will be among the prettiest, but they are the least productive. Lakes surrounded by flat geography tend to be shallow from shore to shore and are often rich in nutrients – the stuff that makes lots of big trout.

Lakes in typical temperate forested terrain have a combination of shallow, sloped shorelines, some shoals removed from the shore, and the limited depths that prevent both warming and winterkill. These are typical trout lakes. They are productive but rarely overpopulated, with a mix of trout from small ones to a few that are large enough to want on the wall.

The bottom composition of a lake is a major physical factor in its productivity. Bedrock doesn't accept rooted vegetation. Sand makes shifty soil and denies plants a firm footing. Both bottom types will be relatively barren. Silt and soft soil make excellent bottoms, holding rooted plants that stand up like underwater forests or that form the dense weed beds that are so productive of insects and beneficial to trout. A black ooze bottom that betrays a thickness of decaying organic debris contains an enormous supply of nutrients. But such a bottom sponsors so much anaerobic bacterial decay that all of the oxygen is used up in the region directly above it, and trout avoid it.

The Three Zones of a Lake

Lakes can be divided into three regions, each with different characteristics, and each with different opportunities for trout – and for trout fishermen.

The *littoral zone* (pronounced the same as literal) is the area of the lake associated with the shoreline, but it also includes any shallows or shoals throughout the lake, not necessarily near the shore. This zone receives the rays of the sun; consequently, it boasts the lake's production of rooted vegetation. Since plants feed insects, and insects feed trout, the littoral zone is the most productive part of any lake that has less than abrupt drop-offs at the shorelines. The littoral zone is where trout spend most of their time during the most productive parts of the trout season. It is where you want to spend most of your time fishing.

The *profundal zone* is the bottom of the lake beyond the limits of light penetration. It is a poor zone in lakes poor in nutrients and with clean bottoms, without much to attract trout. In lakes with lots of nutrient production it is the region where bacterial decay of organic matter takes place. There is little if any oxygen down there. A variety of midge larvae, the bloodworms, have found a

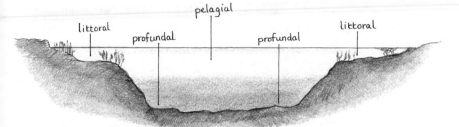

The three major zones of a lake — littoral, profundal, and pelagial — offer different opportunities to the stillwater fisherman.

happy home in the profundal ooze, but trout don't often go into the oxygen-depleted layer after them.

The *pelagial zone* is the open water of the lake, out of association with the shoreline or bottom. It is the home of plankton, which I will discuss in the chapter on plants, although not all plankton are plants. The only aquatic insect that has adapted to pelagic life is the phantom midge *(Chaoborus)*, a small and delicate insect that drifts in open water and uses transparency as camouflage in the larval and pupal stages.

Trout are found in the pelagial zone when they feed on phantom midges, or on midges ascending from the profundal zone for emergence. They are also found there when they feed on plankton, which rainbow do at times, or on schools of baitfish that make a living eating plankton. The largest trout in a lake, the kind that have achieved enough size to depend on baitfish for food, are often found scattered out in the open water of the pelagial region.

Most trout spend most of their time in the littoral zone, however, feeding on the abundance of insects that live on the vegetation prompted by sunlight.

TEMPERATURE, STRATIFICATION, AND TURNOVER

Stratification is a mystifying process until you realize that it is a simple function of water density, which is an equally simple function of water temperature.

Water reaches maximum density — its heaviest weight — at about 39 degrees. Strangely, it gets lighter as it gets either warmer or colder. This is very fortunate in one respect: If water got heavier as it got colder than 39 degrees, lakes would freeze from the bottom up, and they would be more likely to freeze solid. There would be far fewer surviving trout than we have in lakes that now merely ice over.

The annual cycle of stratification and turnover begins in winter, when temperatures in most lakes are nearly the same from top to bottom. This is called winter stagnation. Some lakes stratify under ice, with the coldest water approaching 32 degrees near the surface and the warmest water, approaching 39 degrees and therefore heavier, at the bottom. Whether they stagnate or stratify, there's little difference in water density from top to bottom in winter lakes, and most nutrients settle gently to the bottom. Trout are relatively inactive, partly because what they eat is inactive and partly because the brakes are set on their own metabolisms.

Spring turnover begins when water temperatures, and therefore water densities, begin to rise in the surface layer just after ice-out. Because temperatures from top to bottom are not dramatically different, wind-mixing causes currents that wheel slowly but deep. Nutrients that spent the winter settled on the bottom are stirred up and delivered into all levels of the lake. They are lifted up into the area where sunlight can get at them.

This sudden combination of nutrients and sunlight causes plankton blooms in the pelagial region. In the shallows the same factors spur growth of rooted plants, which causes a surge in activity by aquatic insects and crustaceans. Trout respond to the warmer water and increased food by moving up into shallows and feeding heavily.

Summer stratification begins soon after spring turnover, but it takes a few weeks to establish itself. The sun's energy is absorbed quickly by water, about half of it in the first yard or so at the surface. The top layer warms up quickly, but at first it continues to be mixed with the rest of the water by the wind and the lake currents that are already established by spring winds.

In time the surface layer becomes warm enough to be less dense than the water beneath it. Eventually the difference in density is so great that the lighter water on top cannot penetrate and mix with the heavier water down below. At this point stratification sets in, and a thermocline is developed. The thermocline is a layer of water a few feet thick that displays a sudden drop in temperature. In other words, a sudden rise in density.

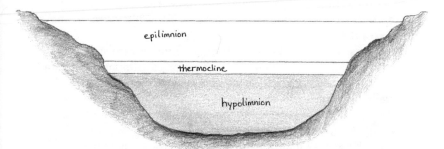

A stratified lake restricts its trout. Knowing where they are in relation to the epilimnion, thermocline, and hypolimnion will help you eliminate a lot of empty water.

During stratification the water settles into three layers: the epilimnion, or warm surface layer; the thermocline, the brief transitional layer; and the hypolimnion, the rest of the cold depths of the lake below the thermocline.

The topmost layer, the epilimnion, continues to be mixed by the wind. Temperatures and nutrient levels remain fairly even at all depths above the thermocline. Because this is the layer where photosynthesis takes place in plankton and plants, oxygen is plentiful. But fresh oxygen is not delivered into the thermocline or the deeper hypolimnion because the differing densities form a barrier to it. That is why most trout are found above the thermocline even in the hottest weather. There's little oxygen for them in it or below it.

Fall turnover begins when the upper epilimnion begins to cool, therefore becoming more dense. As it approaches the temperature of the thermocline, there arrives a time, usually during a fall storm, when the upper layer sinks through the thermocline. This sinking upper layer delivers oxygen to the bottom; it also stirs up the stew of nutrients that have settled there in summer. This is fall turnover, and it always puts a second shot of enrichment into the waters of a lake. It often causes a minor algae bloom before winter stagnation creeps in.

Trout are most active during the periods of turnover. They are most likely to be found feeding in association with plant life in the shallow and rich littoral zone. During stratification they drop toward the thermocline because that is where they find the most comfortable oxygen and temperature levels. But they do this only in lakes that stratify.

Lakes shallower than fifteen to twenty feet rarely stratify because the wind keeps all of the water mixed. In ponds and small lakes with water depths greater than twenty feet the thermocline usually is about ten to fifteen feet deep. In larger lakes the thermocline moves from about thirty feet deep in late spring down to sixty or seventy feet in late summer. The stronger the winds above a lake, the deeper wind-mixing will drive the thermocline.

Cloudy waters sometimes stratify at just five to ten feet because sunlight is absorbed more quickly than it is in clear water. The surface water is a lot warmer, and therefore a lot lighter, than the water a few feet down.

In average temperate lakes – in other words, in average trout waters – the thermocline starts at eight to ten feet deep in late spring and drops to twenty or twenty-five feet by the end of summer. These depths are well within reach with modern sinking-fly lines. But you have to be careful about line selection in order to explore the depth where trout are most likely to be found.

Winterkill is the result of a process that is the opposite of summer stratification. It happens only under ice that is covered with snow, which blocks sunlight and stops the photosynthetic process. This halts the production of oxygen. Clear ice does not block sunlight, and the normal photosynthetic processes are able to continue all winter, supplying oxygen to trout.

Winterkill occurs because the surface water in winter is in contact with the cold atmosphere. When ice forms, the coldest water is at the top; the warmest water, at 39 degrees, is on the bottom. Trout move down deep into the warmer water. But when sunlight is cut off by a layer of snow over the ice, oxygen begins to be depleted down in the dark depths first, because the warmer water there entrains less oxygen than the colder water up toward the top. So trout are forced toward the surface as oxygen dwindles. If snow remains on the ice long enough, the trout move up until they are frozen into the ice or become asphyxiated.

Winterkill almost always happens on shallow lakes with lots of vegetation. Bacterial decomposition of organic debris contributes to oxygen depletion, while the blockage of sunlight halts photosynthesis. Lakes that are deep and poor in nutrients rarely

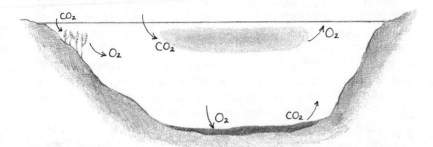

The oxygen/carbon dioxide cycle of a lake is the key element in its chemical structure.

winter-kill because they lack the layer of decomposition in their depths.

CHEMICAL STRUCTURE OF A STILLWATER

The oxygen/carbon dioxide cycle of photosynthesis is the key to the richness of a lake. Rooted plants, attached algae, and phytoplankton all use carbon dioxide and release oxygen. Decomposition of organic material, much of it the decaying remains of plants, uses oxygen and releases carbon dioxide. Sunlight fuels the growth part of the process. Bacteria are the primary organs of decay.

The productivity of this cycle is a function of the nutrients available in a lake. Nitrogen, phosphorus, carbon, and hydrogen are the most important elements in the construction of protoplasm, the living matter of a cell. Calcium is necessary in skeletal structures, such as the bones of trout. Trace elements such as iron and manganese are critical, and at times are limiting.

The "law of the minimum" states that productivity is limited by the least element. In lakes the limiting element is usually phosphorus, nitrogen, or carbon.

Nutrients arrive in lakes from one of three sources. The first is atmospheric exchange through diffusion and by the mixing of wave action. Picture a whitecap driving air into the water. The atmosphere supplies a lake with most of its nitrogen and lots of its oxygen.

The second source of nutrients is incoming water from runoff and tributary streams. Most of the heavy elements are delivered in this manner, and it's quickly obvious that these elements are most likely to be limiting in lakes fed only by seeps; although if the seeps percolate through rich soil, the lakes they feed won't be limited.

The third source of nutrients is decomposition of organic matter in the ooze. Bacterial decay breaks down the complex proteins of dead plants, plankton, insects, and fish, and makes all of their nutrients available for reinsertion into new living matter.

I mentioned that the various structures of a lake are intertwined. The nutrient cycle is a prime example: It is closely linked to the thermal cycle. Nutrients in the less dense and therefore lighter upper layers of a lake where the sun strikes are condensed into a variety of little lives: These are the plankton. These eventually die and slowly filter to the bottom, where they are dismantled by bacteria. But thermal turnover comes along twice a year and stirs the entire stew, returning the free nutrients into the upper layers where they can be assembled into lives again.

It goes on constantly, year after year. Trout are among the largest assemblages of lake nutrients.

We've all heard of the difference between alkaline and acid lakes. Alkaline substances have a positive charge. Lakes rich in them are productive because, reduced to its essence, they have more of the necessary nutrients, primarily carbon compounds, *available in a form useful to life.*

Acidity is a measure of the amount of negatively charged ions in a lake. When a lake is highly acid it has lots of little ions running around to bind up molecules carrying a positive charge. As a result, fewer carbonates are left in available form to compose life.

Acid rain, then, can be understood as man putting extra negative ions into a lake, almost as if pouring them out of a sack. The extra ions tie up carbonates, keep them busy in nonproductive combinations, and reduce their availability as nutrients for the construction of living organisms, including trout and the animals they eat.

Oligotrophic versus Eutrophic

Lakes are divided into two classes, depending on their water chemistry.

Oligotrophic lakes are poor in nutrients, with clear water that allows deep penetration of sunlight. They are usually found in mountainous terrain and have bedrock bottoms. They are deep for their size and, if more than a few acres in extent, have profundal and pelagial zones out of proportion to the rich littoral zone. Plant and planktonic populations are not great because basic nutrients are scarce. Plankton blooms are rare. The bottom tends to be clean due to the lack of organic material. There is seldom that black layer of decaying ooze that is oxygen-poor.

Waters lacking suspended particles to impede light are blue, tending toward blue-green and green as particulate matter increases. Earlier I said that the prettiest lakes are also the poorest. A lake with deep blue water is beautiful to behold, but it lacks the necessary elements to sustain lots of life.

Purely oligotrophic lakes tend to be productive only around the edges.

Eutrophic lakes are shallow and rich in suspended nutrients. Their littoral zones tend to be expansive, reaching far out toward narrow or nonexistent profundal areas. Photosynthesis and lots of nutrients combine to create heavy algal blooms. The abundance of dead and decaying matter filtering down creates a thick and rich ooze that rapidly depletes the oxygen within a yard or two of the bottom.

These shallow lakes tend to form where the geography is old and worn. The lakes themselves are subject to warming and will hold warm-water fish rather than trout if a few thousand feet of altitude or a northerly latitude doesn't protect them from overheating beyond temperatures compatible with trout.

Eutrophic lakes, filled with nutrients that impede light, shift from green toward yellow and even brown as their richness increases. They are not the prettiest to look at, but if conditions are right, they can be the richest to fish.

In geologic terms all lakes are ephemeral, and all are on their way from oligotrophic through eutrophic toward drying marsh and eventual land. This process isn't one you can sit around and watch happen. But in a small water already gone far into eutrophication, it's possible during one's lifetime to watch a pond go from a marginal trout fishery into an excellent warm-water fishery, and perhaps from there get choked with vegetation until you'd hardly want to fish it for anything. I've seen it happen; although in the cases I've witnessed, the process was accelerated by the meddling of man.

POLLUTION AND THE CHEMISTRY OF LAKES

I've already mentioned that acid rain introduces negative ions into the water and binds up the productive nutrients – carbon, nitrogen, phosphorus, and even oxygen – that otherwise would build lives. It's bad.

Fertilizers spread on fields are delivered into lakes by streams and direct runoff. In minute amounts they enrich the water and increase available nutrients. That can be good. But in the types of topographies that are suitable for farming, lakes tend to be shallow and eutrophic already. The added nutrients brought in as fertilizer usually hurt a lake rather than help it. They overenrich it. The increased productivity results in continual algal blooms, choking plant growth, and organic decay that consumes all of the available oxygen. Excess fertilizer can push a trout lake into a warm-water fishery in just a few seasons.

Pesticide runoff has obvious negative effects, as does chemical spray used to kill vegetation rather than fertilize it. Such pollution is killing many of the marginal trout fisheries that exist in farming regions today.

Direct pollution from factory outlets and city sewerage kills a lake either by poisoning it or by overdosing it with nutrients. Both types are tragic, and both are preventable.

3

Plant Life in Lakes

Only a few of the food forms that trout eat are independent of attached vegetative growth of some kind. Zooplankton, the animal forms of plankton, live freely in the pelagial zone and feed on drifting phytoplankton, the plant forms of plankton. Zooplankters are eaten by immature trout of all kinds and by rainbow trout even as adult fish. Many baitfish live on zooplankton and form the intermediate step in the pelagic energy chain that eventually gets condensed into some very large trout.

Phantom midges live in the same pelagial zone, feeding on both zooplankton and phytoplankton. Many other midge forms, especially the bloodworms, live in the oxygen-depleted ooze down in the profundal zone, which is composed of dead material. Very few other trout food forms live independent from rooted vegetation or from minute single- and multicelled plant organisms growing on rocks, woody debris, and shallow bottom silts.

Rooted vegetation itself creates food for insects and crustaceans. But it has an even more important function: It immensely expands the amount of submerged surface area on which minute forms of life, called *periphyton*, can form complicated colonies. The profuse branching and leaf structures of rooted plants form millions of platforms, greatly expanding a surface area that would consist of the flat bottom and nothing more without them.

Periphyton is a microscopic tangle of blue-green, filamentous, and diatomaceous algae, plus about a thousand etceteras all growing together wherever they can find a spot to stand, sit, lie, wiggle, or whatever. You can't see much of it without a microscope. Sometimes it shows up as a slight filmy covering on plants, at other times as a greenish slime. Aquatic insects browse it like cattle in lush fields.

Here's an assignment: The next time you're out on a lake or pond, run your hand along the submerged stem of a cattail, bulrush, or lily pad. Feel how slick it is? That's the periphyton pasture aquatic insects love to browse.

I once captured a *Siphlonurus* mayfly nymph from a pond and put it into a miniature aquarium while I set up my cameras to take its picture. I added a pondweed leaf for the insect to pose on. After I got the camera on its tripod and the extension tubes added to the macro lens, I peered through and it was like looking through a microscope. There was that nymph browsing periphyton on the leaf. It winnowed along with a mouth made for mowing, cutting a swath like a suburbanite pushing a lawn mower. Later, I pickled the poor insect for identification, and felt terrible about it.

ZONES OF PLANT GROWTH

Emergent Vegetation

The first zone of aquatic vegetation is that of plants that stand with their toes in the water but the rest out of it. This is the emergent vegetation. Its aquatic members are fugitives from terrestrial groups and include such well-known rooted plants as bulrushes and cattails. These form dense forests along the shoreline. They are not great habitat for trout unless the stems are separated by some distance, which is not usually the case, since they're packed in tight at their bases. But there's plenty of room in there for aquatic insects, and sometimes even room for trout to maneuver.

The submerged stems of emergent plants make great fields for

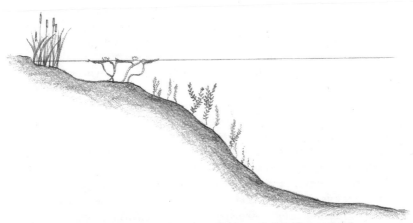

The three zones of aquatic plant growth–rooted, floating, and submerged–all offer different kinds of pastures for insects.

periphyton growth, and the periphyton makes great food for insects. Trout spend lots of time nosing right along the reed edges, picking off strays.

Many aquatics, including damselflies, dragonflies, and some mayflies, must crawl out of the water as nymphs before they can emerge into the world as winged adults. Emergent vegetation, with its submerged stems but aerial stalks, makes the perfect platform for launching such lives. A nymph can crawl right out of the water, take a grip on a stem, split its skin along the back, and exude the bright new adult for the next stage of its short life.

Mating adults often stick around where they started, cruising over the water near the same emergent vegetation fields and falling to the water when it's time to deposit their fertilized eggs. Trout are happy about this. They hang around to applaud with bold swirls.

Floating Vegetation

The next plant zone, just offshore, is the zone of floating vegetation. This includes a variety of arrowheads, lily pads, and spatterdock. All have root systems in the bottom and long trailing stems that reach to the surface. Their leaves float flat on the surface, the bottom side underwater, the top side out of it. The leaves have spiracles that draw air from the atmosphere for respiration.

Duckweed is also a floating plant, but it is a miniature, and its roots hang suspended in the water, taking nutrients directly from the aquatic medium instead of the bottom soil. Duckweed is almost always found in great mats and always close to the shoreline. It can be very rich in aquatic insects.

Stems of floating vegetation create lots of habitat for aquatic nymphs and larvae. Undersides of leaves make even more. Again, periphyton grows profusely on these surfaces and provides lots of feed. The upper sides of the leaves provide perfect emergence platforms. They also form perfect perches for a variety of adults once they've emerged. Damselflies and dragonflies especially seem to prefer sitting in the summer sun on lily pad tops.

Pad flats are best known as bass and panfish habitat. They are a plant of the shallows, where it's often warm, which is why we think of them as hiding warm-water fish and not trout. But many lakes have sufficient altitude or northerly latitude to provide trout-type temperatures and still have lots of emergent vegetation. Trout will spend time, when the temperatures are right, nosing around among the stems of floating vegetation, sometimes even bumping the stems to dislodge aquatic insects.

Submerged Vegetation

The next zone, possibly the most important, is submerged vegetation, which means weed beds. This zone includes the myriad species of pondweed, milfoils, water buttercups, and elodea. It extends from the shore to the limits of light penetration and is dependent on the kind of bottom that allows plants to take root. Bouldery bottoms do not, and sand doesn't encourage rooted plant growth. Rooted aquatic plants do best in a soil bottom that has some firmness.

Weed beds are perhaps the richest pastures in any lake. Stems and leaves increase in fantastic increments the amount of space on which aquatic insects can live, grow, and provide feed for trout. They also provide some shelter for trout deep in their tangled depths, creating a natural nursery and a never-ending supply of insects and other food forms.

Weed beds also make homes for crustaceans, primarily the scuds, which eat the same groceries preferred by aquatic insects. Because they have no hatching cycle, scuds are available to trout all year round. When an insect species is active, it is then more vulnerable to predation, and trout turn to it, sometimes exclusively. But whenever hatches slack off, trout turn back to scuds. They nose right into scattered weed beds. If a weed bed is dense, trout cruise its edges and top, waiting for stray bites to expose themselves to danger.

In addition to providing shelter for insects and crustaceans, weed beds provide shelter for the trout themselves. Trout seek the security of cover whenever they are not out and actively cruising in search of food. They will often rest near a weed bed for the cover of camouflage. They are dark over a dark weed bed and not as exposed as they would be hanging over the open bottom.

In short, trout hang around weed beds to feed. Then they hang around them again to rest. And trout hang around weed beds a lot since that combination of feeding and resting is what they spend most of their time doing.

Planktonic Growth

The final zone of vegetative growth is the pelagial zone. This is the home of the plankton community, which lives without reference to the shore or the bottom.

Plankton is what makes the water look dirty in early spring, and sometimes in cycles repeated throughout the summer and again in fall. If at first glance the water repels you, look more closely and you'll see that it's not dirty, but alive. Most of the forms are too small to see, but many of them reveal themselves to the naked eye or to a magnifying glass held over a sample of water in a white dish or pickle-jar lid.

Phytoplankton is at the base of the pelagic chain. It coalesces nutrients out of the water and gathers them into tiny plants, most of which are microscopic.

Most zooplankton drift freely and ingest any phytoplankton that they encounter by happenstance. More advanced forms propel themselves through the water, seeking out smaller plankters and eating them. Some advanced forms are predaceous and highly

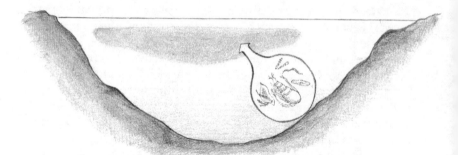

A lot of the energy and nutrients of a lake are condensed into phytoplankton and zooplankton, which are indirectly converted into fuel for
trout.

motile. They seek out smaller zooplankters, attacking and ingest-
ing them. These larger and more active forms are the ones most
likely to be fed on by small trout, and even by larger rainbows,
when plankton finds itself in the trout diet.

Individual plankters are slightly more dense than water. They
are held suspended in the water column by the same force that
disperses energy through it in the temperature cycle: currents
generated by wind, which scientists call eddy diffusion. It is the
same force that keeps dust motes suspended and circulating in a
room full of air. As you can readily perceive, it doesn't take much
force to accomplish the constant circulation of living plankton in
a lake.

When plankton dies, it settles slowly to the bottom, where it
becomes fuel for bacterial decay in the profundal ooze. Eventually
it becomes nutrients once again in the stew that is stirred by spring
and fall turnover.

SHAPE OF A WEED BED

How does all of this stuff about plant growth translate into practi-
cal fishing terms? My dad and I just got back from a four-day
fishing trip to a forested mountain lake, a trip that might illuminate the subject a little.

The lake was just over twenty acres, on the east flank of the
Cascade Mountains at 4,000 feet, full of rainbow trout that fail to

grow large because an excellent spawning tributary contributes an excess of fry to it. There's not much fishing pressure to prune the population. You're encouraged to keep trout there, and we did, so I was able to study lots of stomach samples.

The lake had emergent reeds along some of the shoreline. The stems harbored lots of mayfly nymphs and cased caddis larvae but weren't much of a factor in the fishing. In most areas the lakeshore sloped gradually up to the reeds, and by the time it got to them was only a foot or so deep. Apparently trout weren't comfortable going into water so thin and clear that the osprey occasionally circling overhead would have an easy shot at them. That is speculation on the trout's reasons for not working the reeds; at another time they might have risked it. But not while Dad and I were there.

The next zone of vegetation, floating plants, was missing entirely. There were no lily pads, no arrowheads or duckweed flats.

The third zone, that of plants rooted in the bottom, took two forms. The first was the typical bunched and clearly bordered weed bed. These condensed beds grew along one side of the lake in water five to ten feet deep and varied from small patches the size of a desk top to larger beds ten to fifteen feet wide and up to thirty feet long. They grew in tight masses like frizzed haircuts, two to three feet thick and tight against the bottom. You can imagine the number of tiny organisms such a mass of vegetation might contain.

The second form of rooted plants was harder to spot. I became aware of it in a peculiar way – while drifting lazily over water eight to ten feet deep, looking idly over the side because fishing was slow at the moment. I noticed a sort of zebra striping on the white silty bottom. It was scattered with short black lines, but they were all straight and parallel. When I finally focused on them, what I discovered was interesting: The black lines were the shadows of plants that were so spindly and transparent that they were almost invisible. Only their shadows showed.

These rooted plants, probably some sort of pondweed, were only one to two feet tall and were sprinkled a foot or two apart across acres of bottom. Each stalk had a single stem with about a dozen leaves climbing up it. These scattered plants did not form a dense weed bed, but the increase in forage area that they created

When you locate weedbeds, which often appear only as mysterious darkenings on the surface of the lake, you have usually located trout.

made millions of homes for cased caddis larvae and led to some interesting fishing for Dad and me.

We fished from prams, sometimes drifting with the wind and casting at random, sometimes dropping anchor and exploring a place thoroughly when one or two fish hit our random casts. A pattern began to work itself out after a couple of days on the lake.

The dense weed beds were hard to locate except when the wind was still, which was seldom, and the sun struck down into the water just right to illuminate the bottom. For a couple of days we failed to get them patterned. But on the third day conditions got just right, weed beds showed up all over as dark blotches on the bottom, and we were able to anchor off at a respectable distance, then lay our flies right over them. We used #12 Olive Woolly Buggers with their trailing marabou tails pinched short; we'd seen scattered olive dragonfly nymphs in earlier stomach samples.

Wet-tip lines helped get the flies down a few feet, but it wasn't necessary to get them clear down to the beds. The trout seemed very willing to come up and attack them. The important thing was to get the fly into the proximity of a weed bed, give it some time to sink, then retrieve it at a creeping rate. Not every cast produced a fish. But every bed did, and some produced three or four.

The scattered forest of weeds over the broader bottom presented a different kind of fishing. We caught just as many trout there, perhaps more. But they were spread out, obviously cruising rather than holding, and we did better by wind-drifting and casting, or even by trolling slowly, than we did by anchoring and casting.

The tactic was nearly the same: cast out, let the fly sink, then retrieve it slowly. But the fly and the reasons it worked were different.

These sparse weeds sponsored a population of vegetation-cased caddis in the family Leptoceridae. The larvae look exactly like tiny sticks. But they have a uniqueness: they're swimming sticks. They stick their six little legs out the front of the case and use them to winnow their way slowly through the water, about like you'd swim if your legs were tied together in a sleeping bag.

We caught trout after trout stuffed with these stick cases, the nutritious caddis worms already digested out of them. Our fly was what I'll call a Bugger because it was an Olive Woolly Bugger but without any "woolly." I tied them in the tent on short-shank #12 hooks but left off the hackle.

The same lake had just one bed of milfoil, the tufted and many-branched weed that looks like a tangle of the tails of a thousand frightened cats. This bed was a twenty-foot oval. One side was contiguous with shore, but the outside edge grew about five feet up from a ten-foot bottom in a sort of cliff face that went down into dark water. This bed was a natural lake lie for a large trout, as clearly defined as a streambed boulder in the middle of a deep run.

The largest trout Dad and I took, on each circuit of the lake for four days, always came up along that dark cliff of submerged vegetation.

Part II
Strategies for Stillwaters

4

Gearing Up for
Lakes and Ponds

I can give you an example of the benefits of owning the right tackle
and knowing how to use it well. My dad and I fished out of
separate prams one day. The air was still, the water was clear, and
the trout were shy of our boats. They cruised the water column
and would take at any depth between one and five feet down. But
they wouldn't follow a fly and strike it inside a circle about thirty
feet around each boat.

Outside of that circle they were eager for our flies.

Dad cast with an 8-foot rod, a graphite strung with a line one
size too light to load the rod well. He has always fished small
streams, no more than twenty feet across, and has always considered a forty-foot cast half wasted. As an understandable consequence he hasn't honed his casting stroke in order to get much
punch out of any rod. And with modern graphite rods, if you don't
load them, they won't fire.

Most of Dad's casts propelled his fly thirty-five or forty feet
from the boat, just beyond the edge of that circle surrounding him
within which no fish would hit because they were boat shy. He did

well enough. But I'll thump my chest and tell you I did lots better, for an easy reason.

I'm no great caster. Most of my trout are taken with nymphs or wet flies fished close, or with dry flies fished on short casts into fading rise-rings. But I was using an 8½-foot rod that day, a strong one, and I've fished often enough for summer steelhead, for bass off in the distance, and for trout in lakes, that I've learned to make a fly rod bend deeply and spring forward to toss line. I've learned to make the rod do the work. There are books about how to do it, including my own *Tackle & Technique*. If you don't know how, I'd recommend that you learn. Loading a rod correctly makes casting sixty feet easy, which is what I was doing.

Reducing trout fishing to geometry seems a stinky thing to do, but for a moment I'm going to do it. If you subtract the area of a thirty-foot fishless circle around a boat from that of a forty-foot circle, you get about 2,000 square feet of water left that holds fish willing to strike a fly. That is the size of the effective area Dad fished with his average cast. But subtract that same thirty-foot fishless circle from a larger sixty-foot circle, and you wind up with about 8,500 square feet of area that is likely to hold willing trout. By casting just twenty feet farther I was able to cover more than four times as much water with the potential to provide an angry trout.

If you think I'm bragging, forget it. I fish with friends all the time who cast eighty feet, which gives them twice the water that I fish with my sixty-foot casts. And it shows in their results: They catch twice the trout I do. I won't tell you their names. It would go to their heads.

FLY RODS

It seems that fly rods always come up first in any discussion about fly-fishing tackle, while fly lines are truly the heart of the matter, especially when the subject is stillwater fishing. But let's stick with tradition and look at rods before looking at lines to load them.

Length for a lake rod is simple: There's no reason for a short one unless you just contrarily want one. The longer the rod, the longer your lever, and the higher you can hold your backcast off the water. All this, of course, is subject to reason. To me, 8½ to 9½ feet is within reason, although more folks are now going to rods 10 to 10½ feet long for lake fishing. There's no reason not to, as long as the rods are light and responsive. Fiberglass, bamboo, and even some early graphite rods that long would kill you after a short time spent casting. When fishing lakes it's common to do lots of casting.

The goal is more often distance than delicacy in lake fishing for trout. At times it's distance with delicacy added at the end. The new generation of graphite rod materials, which are often too stiff for short casts and soft presentations, become excellent when you want to use a long rod to cast a tight loop and punch a line far out, or into a wind.

Such fast rods are great for lakes if they suit your casting style. With a short, crisp stroke they are able to turn over a long, tight line. That adds up to distance with ease, but the same distance can be achieved with a moderate-action rod, or even a slow one. What the ease achieves is a slight saving of energy on each cast. That offers you a longer, more pleasant day alake.

But no rod is going to give you much pleasure if it doesn't suit your casting style. Stick with a moderate rod if that is what you've always used. And stick with a moderate rod if that's what you already own and use. Never rush out and buy a rod until a desire for something specific has announced itself. That way, when you do buy one, you'll know exactly what you want.

The rod you want might be different from the rod I want.

I usually use two rods for lake fishing if the situation allows me to carry them, which means when I'm fishing out of a boat. I recommend that you consider doing the same. It's an approach toward the tournament bass fisherman's battery of rods, and I've known trout fishermen to fish with three or four rods rigged up in the boat. There's nothing wrong with that, except that I'd get tangled up in them and confused by them. I keep my own selection to a couple of rods handy at one time.

The first rod is for light-line fishing over feeding trout, usually with dry flies or with nymphs fished just beneath the surface. But it's also useful for casting small streamers or small weighted nymphs that are to be fished relatively shallow. The rod that I use for this purpose is an 8-footer for a 5-weight line, primarily because it's my favorite rod, and it leaps into my hand whenever I reach for a rod when preparing to go fishing. If I were to choose a

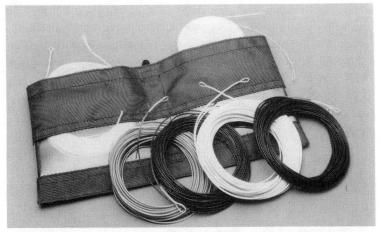

A shooting-head system makes it easy to change the depth fished quickly, without restringing the rod. *Orvis, Inc.*

new rod just for this one kind of lake and pond fishing, it would be 8½ to 9 feet long and would balance to a 5-weight line. If I lived in country that was less windy, it would be a 4-weight rather than the heavier 5-weight.

This rod always starts off strung with a double-taper floating line. But I carry a spare spool wound with a weight-forward wet-tip line and switch to it whenever I want to get my fly a few feet down, which is often.

The second rod is for what I call system fishing. It's an 8½-footer for 7-weight lines. I use it to carry heavy nymphs and large streamers out to long range, and to buck winds. But these are not its main missions. What it's designed to do is cast a series of shooting-head lines with different sink rates so I can explore all the depths a lake might offer.

Some years ago I purchased a set of four shooting heads from a major line maker. One of them goes on the reel, the rest of them nest in a folding wallet, coiled up and out of the way in my vest. Whenever the situation changes, it's easy to remove the line I'm using and loop on one of a different sink rate. Because it's not necessary to change reel spools, the operation can be done beyond the rod tip and doesn't entail restringing the rod, which can be difficult in a small boat, and an adventure in a float tube.

Again, the 8½-foot rod I use for this purpose is shorter than what I would choose if this were its only purpose. I contrarily choose rods about half a foot shorter than the rods I recommend. If I were to choose one specifically for handling my shooting-head system on stillwaters, it would be a 9-footer, and it would be made of one of the latest generation graphites for lightness, quickness, and the tightness of its casting loops.

LINES

I use a floating line more than any other for a couple of reasons. First, I try to make my trips to lakes during periods when trout are actively feeding up toward the top. Second, I fish nymphs most often with a slow retrieve. Weight on the fly often gives me the depth I need, and the floating-line tip serves as a strike indicator.

When trout feed visibly, with swirls on the surface that indicate takes on top or just under it, then a floating line will obviously deliver your fly exactly where you want it. When trout feed a foot or so down, you can use a dry line to show them an unweighted fly at that depth, and you're left the advantage of a visible tip for an indicator, which you would lose by going to a wet-tip line.

When trout feed deeper, down to three or four feet, a weighted fly attached to a long leader and floating line can still achieve the right level. Tie it to the end of a 3- to 4-foot tippet that is as fine as you dare and give the fly some time to sink. Again, you retain the advantage of the visible tip.

For lake fishing it would seem that the weight-forward floater would be better than a double taper. But I find myself using a double taper most often because that's what's on the reel that goes with my favorite rod, which I use equally on streams, where I prefer the control of the double taper. But more important, the floating line is used often in stillwater situations where trout rise sporadically all around, making their internal feeding movements inside the larger movements in an area or within a moving school. It's an advantage to be able to pick up the line and fly quickly, make a change-of-direction cast in the air, and place the fly gently near the latest rise.

A weight-forward taper must be drawn in at least close to the heavy casting portion of the line before you can lift it and cast again with any degree of control. That costs time while the trout moves away from its rise. Then you have to lift the weight-forward line from the water with a pull straight toward the rod, which is the right way to do it most of the time. But when trout rise all around you, lifting the fly off this way can cause a disturbance that they fail to appreciate. They'll often move off with disapproving backward glances.

With a double-taper line you can roll the after portion into the air, pick up the front portion with much less disturbance, make your change of direction quickly, and lay the fly back out lightly. It is similar to the advantage you receive from a double-taper line on moving water: There you have more control of the line on the water. In stillwater fishing you have more control of the line in the air.

The weight-forward gives the advantage of some slight increase in distance with some slight decrease in effort. If I'm casting for distance, I use it, which means that whenever I switch to a wet-tip line I also switch from a double taper to a weight-forward taper. I use a weight-forward whenever I'm casting with anything but a light rod, since the goal is again more likely to be distance than delicacy, and the weight-forward delivers it. Most rods load properly with a weight-forward line one size heavier than the double taper they handle best. This is subject to rod power and your casting stroke. You should be sure to try the line for which your rod is rated, as well as the next size up, before deciding which one to buy.

I use bright fluorescent floating lines for stillwater fishing, but sometimes I wish I didn't. They have the advantage of being highly visible, and the tip makes a fine strike indicator, which is why I use them. But they are somewhat intrusive in the environment, and there's little doubt that trout sometimes see them flashing in the air. A white line lying on the water is least visible against the sky from underneath where the trout cruise. A dark floating line is opaque on the surface and is most visible to trout. I suspect fluorescent lines fall somewhere in between. I know that trout are not often spooked by them on the water, although they'll flee from the sight of any line flying over them in the air.

Your floating line should always be cleaned with line dressing before you begin fishing. If the lake or pond is cloudy with either silt or an algae bloom, then clean it several times during the day.

Keep the line slipping easily through the guides and your casting will be easier, your fishing more fun.

A wet-tip line with a 10-foot section up front that sinks is extremely useful on lakes and ponds. Its primary use is to get a fly down into the three- to five-foot range where trout often feed, especially when they cruise along sloped shorelines or hold over shallow weed beds. It's great for that, and you can keep your fly traveling at just the right depth when you use a slow to moderate retrieve. But a wet-tip line is also great for fishing streamers shallow with a fast-stripping retrieve.

When you fish a fly fast, the most common problem is having it ride up into the surface film, where it leaves a wake and spooks the fish. You can let it sink, but the speed of the retrieve causes it to plane upward again. Weight will solve the problem to a certain extent, but it's not the entire solution because you don't want to fling all that lead about, and also because you don't want to tie your #10 Olive Woolly Buggers in versions that are lightly weighted for slow retrieves, moderately weighted for average retrieves, and heavily weighted for racing retrieves. Life is confusing enough; weight all of your Woolly Buggers the same.

By using a wet-tip line you insure that your sunk flies remain sunk no matter how fast the retrieve, no matter how lightly the fly is weighted. It's an advantage of the line that is often overlooked.

Wet tips come in a couple of sink rates from most manufacturers. Both are useful, but for lakes I tend to skip the slow sink rate and go right to the fastest, since it allows me to go shallow by starting the retrieve as soon as the fly lands on the water. It also gives me the option of being more patient and getting down deeper. The fact that I can carry one spare spool rather than two helps; I get cranky when my burden of gear becomes too great.

An intermediate line can solve some of the same problems. It is designed to sink very slowly and stay just under the surface. It also keeps a fly underwater on a fast retrieve, and keeps the line out of the way of wind-drift, which can be a problem on many lakes when you fish a floating line.

An intermediate line has the advantage, as opposed to the wet-tip line, of having no hinge. A wet tip sinks with an angle at the junction of the floating and sinking portions, and another at the junction of leader and line. These cause some delay in the way you

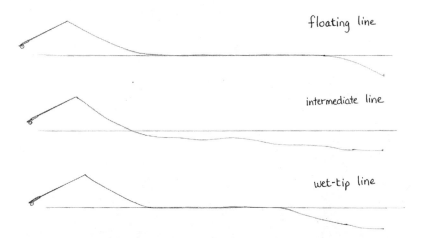

You can fish a fly at the same level with floating, intermediate, or wet-tip lines, but each has its own way of getting the fly down there.

get told of a take, and there's no question a few fish are lost because they've let go of the fly before you get the news.

The intermediate draws a straight line between the rod tip and the fly. When you want to fish one or two feet deep, and don't mind carrying an extra line to do the job, then it's the best way to go. If you fish in a lot of situations where the line would be an advantage, then you should have one. But other lines will fish at the same depth with some slight compromise: the dry, which is subject to wind-drift; or the wet tip, which is subject to hinges. The intermediate has the disadvantage of sinking its entire length, which means you have to pull the entire line out of the water, rather than lifting it off the surface, for each cast.

Floating, wet-tip, and intermediate lines solve the shallow problems. I use them all the time with my light rod and quite a bit of the time with my heavier rod. But the remaining problem – the larger one on lakes – is how to explore the remaining depths.

Three systems solve the problem of depth in different ways. The goal is to be able to sink your fly to various levels, and to keep it there throughout the retrieve with some amount of control and some hope of getting a report quickly if you get a hit.

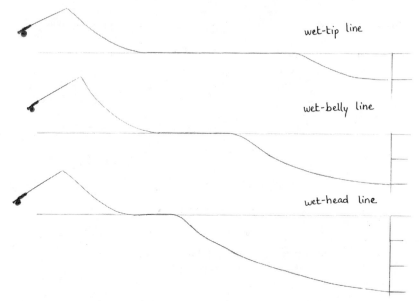

wet-tip line

wet-belly line

wet-head line

A system of wet-tip, wet-belly, and wet-head lines lets you explore the various levels of a lake.

The Floating/Sinking Solution

Modern fly lines are a miracle; you can buy them to float, buy them to sink, or buy one line that does both. The end section of the line plummets, but the running line behind it floats. By using floating/sinking lines in various configurations you can cover most of the depths where trout are found feeding.

This system for fishing all the depths starts with a floating line, as all of the systems do. You have to be able to present dry flies and shallow wets or nymphs. The floater should be your first line, not necessarily because you'll use it most often, but because it can be used to fish both the top and the first foot or two under it, thereby serving the functions of a couple of lines.

The second line in the floating/sinking system is one that I've already mentioned: the wet tip. It has ten feet of sinking line ahead of the floating running line. In the fast-sink rate it can cover the depths from three to five feet down. That's a lot of water, since a trout holding ten feet deep might willingly dash up five feet to intercept an enticing fly.

The third line should be a wet belly, with 20 feet of sinking line ahead of the floating running line. This line will fish a fly in the area between five and ten feet deep, again if it's chosen in the fast-sink rate.

The fourth and final line in the floating/sinking system is the wet head, with a full 30 feet of sinking line. In the normal weight-forward taper this is the entire heavy portion of the line. The wet head will fish the depths from ten feet down to twenty.

With all of the floating/sinking combinations the depth fished can be controlled by the amount of weight on the fly, by the length of time the line is given to pull the fly down, and by the speed of the retrieve once it gets there. A heavily weighted fly, given a long count and a hand-twist retrieve, will fish a few feet deeper than the rated depth for a wet tip, wet belly, or wet head. A fly that is lightly weighted and retrieved at a trot the second it touches the water will not fish very deep no matter what line you use.

The advantages of the floating/sinking line system for exploring depths are the simplicity of the four line types and the ease of casting them. They should all be weight-forwards, and all should cast without problems if you keep the floating part of the line dressed. Don't ever dress the sinking portion or you'll cause them to try to float.

The disadvantages of this system are the number of spare reel spools you have to inventory and carry, and the hinges in the line at the junction of floating and running sections, and again at the tip of the line and the butt of the leader. In addition, when you retrieve fast after the fly has reached the depth you want, the floating part of the line will cause the fly to rise up in the water. Rather than a level retrieve at a chosen depth, your fly rises. It won't do this on a slow retrieve.

When using all but the floating line in this system, keep your leaders short: four to six feet. There is no use getting your line down and then letting a long leader hold your fly far up above it.

Full-sinking Lines

The oldest way to explore all of the depths in a lake is to carry a range of full-sinking lines in various sink rates. This system still has its advantages, although like all the systems, it has disadvantages, too.

This system begins, again, with the floating line. The next logical line is the intermediate, which gets just under the water, but you have to decide how much you'll use it and how many lines you want to carry. For purposes of experimentation I recommend that you try it. Many experts at fishing lakes consider it a mandatory line. I don't.

Next in this system is a slow-sinking line, to get down three to five feet. This is also an excellent line for fishing streamers shallow on a fast retrieve. It keeps them from breaking up through the surface.

The depths from five to ten feet are fished in this system with a fast-sinking line. Below that, from ten to twenty feet, an extra-fast sinker delivers the fly down and keeps it there with a relatively patient retrieve. Ultrafast-sinking lines are available to get the fly down to the greatest depths, which will let you fish in the area of the thermocline in most lakes.

The greatest advantage of the full-sinking line is the level retrieve that it allows, without any hinges, since all the line sinks at about the same rate. This is not an idle matter. Once you've started your retrieve at a certain depth, the fly will ride out the retrieve at the same depth without rising or sinking. You can count the fly down to a weed bed and draw it back, fast or slow, right above the weed bed.

There are some disadvantages to the full-sinking line system. You have to carry a spare reel spool for each line. You have to lift all of the line out of the water each time you cast, since none of it floats. And if you're wading or fishing from a float tube, this gets to be quite a problem.

I fish a favorite lake by log-hopping a lot; the shoreline is strewn with floating logs large enough to walk on, if I'm careful, which isn't always. I won't detail my misadventures on these logs, but I will tell you that a full-sinking line, when brought in on the retrieve and dropped next to the log, will sink and coil around every limb. I'll give you a vision: Can you see me down on my knees, my butt in the air and my nose in the water, probing around with my rod tip?

I don't do that anymore. The place for the full-sinking system is in a boat that has enough floor room to hold all of your running line.

When using full-sinking lines it makes sense to use them in weight-forward tapers, since the farther you can get them out, the longer retrieve you can get with the fly at the depth you want to fish.

Shooting-head Systems

Shooting heads are sections of level line, the length being 25 to 35 feet, the weight being what it takes to balance the appropriate rod rating. You can make your own, cutting sections out of level, double-taper, or even weight-forward lines. But it's cheapest just to buy the heads already made up.

I bought a whole system of four heads, each looped at both ends for the running line and leader. They range from floating through intermediate to fast sinking and ultrafast, and cover the depths from the top to twenty feet. The running line I use is level and is very thin floating fly line. You can also get braided running line or use monofilament, but you will have to deal with a lot more tangles.

The shooting-head system has some advantages that make it attractive to me. Each line is kept coiled in a wallet, and the entire system in its wallet takes up about the same amount of room in my vest that a single spare reel spool would take. When I want to change heads, I don't have to reel the line through the guides, switch spools, then restring the rod. All I have to do is unloop one head, coil it up, uncoil the new head, and loop it on. I don't even have to change flies when I'd like to fish the same one at a different depth. It's easy to take the leader off the old line and loop it onto the new one. I'm back in business in a hurry, which to me is always important.

Disadvantages of the shooting-head system are serious. The thin running line, even if it's coated fly line, tends to tangle more frequently than the thicker running line behind a weight-forward taper. A shooting head has hinges, changing depth abruptly where the running and sinking lines meet, and less abruptly where the line and leader join. The loops do not go through the guides on the retrieve as smoothly as line without loops. This can cause you to think that you've had a strike when you haven't – and feel is so much a part of fishing a sunk fly.

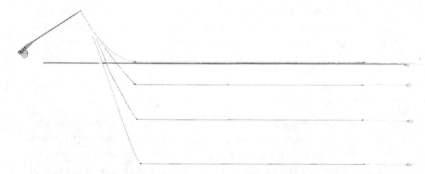

A shooting-head system has some hinges in it, but most of the disadvantages are outweighed by the advantage of convenience in carrying the setup.

The deep retrieve of a shooting-head system is not level; the floating running line tends to hitch it toward the surface. This is not as dramatic as it is with a floating/sinking line because the sinking part of a head far outweighs the thin running line. But it is a factor; on a fast retrieve the fly will climb.

It's hard to attain perfection and still be able to carry the equipment you need to achieve it. I strive for simplicity in my gear so I'm likely to have it with me when I need it. That's why I carry a shooting-head system for searching the various levels of lakes: It's easy to tuck into a pocket in my vest or a corner of my boat bag.

LEADERS

The leader serves three functions. It separates the line from the fly with a connection that is theoretically invisible to the trout. It transfers the energy of the cast from the line down to the fly, laying it out straight. And, when fishing the dry fly it gives the fly some freedom to float naturally.

To perform these functions the leader must be reasonably long and should be tapered from a stout stern down to a fine tippet.

On stillwater you're always fishing over the equivalent of a flat in a stream. Leader length for the average lake-fishing situation should be 10 to 12 feet, a couple of feet longer than the average on moving water. Two to 3 feet of that length should be tippet. It's amazing to me how often I shorten my tippet by changing flies or losing them and find strikes dwindling to nothing, then refresh my tippet to its normal length and discover that trout are suddenly there and eager again.

If the lake is wind-riffled and trout are taking dries, the leader can be shorter. Because wind makes long leaders quarrelsome, shortening the leader and cutting the tippet to a couple of feet will be worthwhile.

When fishing dries over fish that are fussy and a lake surface that is calm, you'll have to extend the leader. It's always best to do this at the tippet end, not in the midsections or at the butt. Add a 2-foot section in the first diameter behind the tippet, then extend the tippet itself. The leader should be 12 to 15 feet long.

With a leader this long you have to tend to your casting. Make sure the leader turns over and extends beyond the line at the end of each cast. It's easy to try for too much distance and get the leader piled up, or blown back behind the line by the slightest breeze. If that starts happening, it's better to shorten the casts to those you can control, or else shorten the leader so it turns over nicely again.

There's no use stacking the longest and finest leader on top of your line tip. No trout will agree to sort out the mess to find the fly.

When you fish sinking lines, whether they are wet tips, full sinkers, or shooting heads, shorten your leaders to between 4 and 6 feet. For most of my fishing I buy 10-foot tapered leaders and add tippets to suit the situation. But for wet-line fishing I just tie a 2-foot butt of about .021 inches or .019 inches, add a 1- or 2-foot midsection of about .011 to .015 inches, then a tapering section a foot long that splits the difference in diameter between the midsection and whatever I'm going to use for a tippet.

There are exceptions to the rule for short leaders at the end of sinking or sink-tip lines. I've seen times when trout were cagey, especially in clear water, and kept away from flies fished on short leaders. The addition of three to four feet of fine tippet always seems to solve the problem, although you then have to be more patient getting the fly down to depth. It also helps to slow the retrieve so the fly will keep the depth you've so patiently attained.

Whenever you fish a weighted fly with a dry line and want some depth, the best way to achieve it is by extending the leader. This should always be done by lengthening the tippet and the section behind it. The finer tippet follows the fly down without impeding its sink rate. If you try to achieve depth by lengthening the midsections or butt of the leader, the thicker stuff won't allow the fly the freedom it needs to sink.

Size of the tippet should be relative to the size fly you are casting. See the accompanying chart for rough equivalents between fly and leader size. It works best to keep the balance within these parameters in order to get the best leader turnover. If the leader is too light for the fly, the cast will crumble. If the leader is too stout, it will smack the fly to the water.

"X"	Diameter	Fly Size
1X	.011	1/0, 1, 2
2X	.010	4, 6, 8
3X	.008	10, 12, 14
4X	.007	12, 14, 16
5X	.006	14, 16, 18, 20
6X	.005	18, 20, 22, 24
7X	.004	20, 22, 24, 26

Leader strength is often a compromise between the slenderness it takes to fool trout and the strength it takes to hold them. This is relative to water clarity, trout selectivity, the size and fight of the fish, and the presence of nearby difficulties such as weed beds or limb tangles that will snap fragile tippets.

Not long ago on Washington's Nunnally Lakes chain I encountered some rainbow trout that were enormously fussy, cruising in calm water that did not impede sight, broad shouldered enough to cause problems once they got attached to a hook. But I had problems getting them attached until I dropped the tippet down to 6X, about 3-pound test. Then I managed to hook quite a few, but almost every one bolted like a bonefish, dropped over a ledge, and shot off through a bed of sparse pondweed.

It wasn't sparse enough. The leader tangled every time and put

Landing a fat trout requires that the leader be fine enough to fool the fish, but stout enough to hold it. Sometimes the right balance is difficult to find.

on its own brakes, but the trout kept on dashing. As far as I know, they're still going.

Leader kinks—retention of the coils that the monofilament takes while stored on narrow spools—can cost you fish, especially when you fish sunk flies. If the leader is not straight, when a fish takes the fly it has all that room to run before the kinks come out and the take gets reported up the line to you. Make sure you straighten your leader before you cast it. Just stretch it between your hands, which also tests your knots, and hold it a few seconds. If that doesn't do it, draw it between the folds of a piece of inner tube or a commercial leader straightener.

Be sure to carry leader and tippet materials from the same manufacturer. Different brands are weak where they're joined at knots, and this results in trout swimming away trailing long lengths of tippet, which isn't good for the trout or your temper.

I carry 2X and 3X tippet spools for use in rebuilding the end tapers of my store-bought leaders or the midsections of my hand-tied leaders. I use 4X through 6X spools constantly. I also carry a spool of 7X, but rarely use it.

I've been using knotless leaders lately, bought in 7½-, 10-, and

13-foot lengths. My most common dry fly leader is a 10-footer added to a 2-foot butt section that's permanently on the end of my fly line. That gives me a 12-foot leader, which I can lengthen with finer tippet if needed. When I fish a sinking line, I often use a 7½-foot commercial leader, sometimes cutting it back, sometimes leaving it the way it is until it gets cut back by natural attrition.

REELS

There isn't much to say about reels except to emphasize that they should be single action not automatics, and they should have fine drags. Trout in lakes and ponds are often larger and heavier than those found in rivers and streams. Some are hot and make bold runs when stung by a hook. You want a reel that will surrender line to the run without stuttering or seizing up.

The reel should be in balance with the size of the rod, both aesthetically and in weight. A big blocky reel on a slim graphite rod looks bad, although it might fish well. And a reel that is too heavy makes casting a bit of a chore: Its extra ounces niggle at your elbow and wrist until you get worn down and sore.

Any reel used in trout fishing, on moving water or still, should hold the line plus 100 yards of backing. You'll rarely need that much – a trout a hundred yards away is truly a long way out there, almost out of touch – but backing gives you time to get your anchor up and get after a fast-moving fish if you need to. It also helps fill the reel spool, which means you'll retrieve the maximum amount of line with each twirl of the reel handle. If you've ever tried to catch up with a trout swimming fast toward you, and your spool is so thin that you're gaining only an inch or two with each crank, you'll know what panic is all about.

A reversible reel helps. You'll want the choice between right- and left-hand wind. Most smart right-handed folks that I fish with set their reels up to crank with the left hand so they can fight fish with the rod in their right hand. I use reels the way they come from the manufacturer, for right-hand retrieve, but there are times when I wish I didn't. Those times almost always come when I'm playing a fish the size I hate to lose. Switching the rod from hand to hand becomes somewhat awkward, but I continue to do it because I haven't gotten used to reeling the other way. It's a mistake you don't need to make.

Any reel you buy should give you the option of buying spare spools. If it doesn't, don't buy it. You will want to carry one with a dry line, another with a wet tip. If you use floating/sinking lines to fish the various depths of stillwaters, you'll need a spare spool for each separate line. The same is true if you choose to explore the depths with a range of full-sinking lines. Even if you use a shooting-head system, you'll want a spare spool or two so you can experiment with one of the other line types from time to time.

FLY BOXES

It's best to carry your flies separated according to their kind: dries, wets, nymphs, and streamers. That way it's easier to find what you're after.

I used to take this to an extreme, using cough-drop boxes and medicine tins to isolate Alders from Cahills and Woolly Buggers from Black and Uglies. But I found myself carrying so many little fly boxes that, even with labels, I had to pat myself down to find the one I wanted. Now I've gone to the other extreme.

A box that contains flies based on lake food forms, all of them dressings that have fished well for you, will prove itself remarkably valuable over the years.

I try to carry all my dry flies in one box with lots of separate compartments. All streamers go into a streamer box with ridged foam inserts. Wet flies go into another foam box, and nymphs into a third. Now when I want a particular fly, I have less inventorying to do before I find it. It works well, although the boxes are beginning to spill over. I'll soon need another dry-fly box, an extra streamer box and nymph box, and so on.

If you're like me and fish lakes and ponds at times but fish rivers and streams at least as often, there's one special box that's worth considering. This box is especially helpful for tramps to ponds or lakes where you want to keep your luggage to a minimum. I've labeled mine the "lake box," and have filled it with the flies that work on stillwater most often.

The contents of this box are based on the most common lake food forms, since that is what trout eat most often and are most pleased to see. It contains drys for the *Callibaetis* mayflies, wets for the alderflies, nymphs for damsel- and dragonflies, and streamers to match leeches. Of course, the list goes on and on, and the box is filled to overflowing. But when I hike to a lake or pond, even one I've never fished before, I have a fair degree of confidence that the fly I need will reside in my lake fly box.

VESTS AND ACCESSORIES

You can view vests for stillwater fly-fishing in a couple of different ways. The first view sees the vest as a tackle pack: It carries everything you might need for a day on a lake. When used this way the vest should be of the full-length type, with lots of pockets in varying sizes to hold all of your fly boxes, thermometers, nippers, and etceteras. It will weigh heavily in the hand, and perhaps on the neck. It will get wet around the bottom rim whenever you wade deep or hold your nose and leap into a float tube. But it won't let you down when you want to look up an obscure item.

The other way to view the vest is as a vehicle for the most common necessities, to which you can add whatever specific items you feel you might need on a given day. The vest for this kind of fishing should be a shortie or midlength and should still have lots of pockets, although it won't have as many as a full-length vest because there isn't as much room for them. The shorter vest will let you wade deep or dangle yourself from a float tube without getting fly boxes wet. There will be times, unless you're a lot smarter than I am, which I assume you are, that you'll forget an item or two that's needed.

But it's a trade-off: forever burdened or occasionally forgetful? I choose the latter.

The accessories that I always carry in the vest don't weigh much or take up much room. When I want to flesh it out for the day, I look through my various fly boxes and decide which ones I might want for the kind of fishing I'll be doing. I also look through various added attractions and decide what additional accessories I might want for the day, such as a water bottle or pocket camera and film.

Those are choices I need to make every time I go fishing. To help myself out, to make sure I have them available on a trip and get to look at each one and either take it or leave it, I've added a boat bag to my collection of necessary fishing gear.

Inventory of the author's vest:
Handkerchief. Indicators and split shot. Line dressing. Leader tippets in 2X to 7X. Fly floatant. Sunglasses. Toilet paper. Thermometer. Nippers on retriever. Mosquito repellent. Insect kit: vials, jar lid, magnifying glass. Hemostat. Aquarium net. Spare leaders in 7½, 10, and 13 feet.

THE BOAT BAG

I use a large Wood River bag to hold all of the things I might want but don't want to carry every time I go fishing. I keep the bag in the car. If I launch a boat, it goes into the boat. It doesn't take up much room, and there's no reason to limit any of my possibilities unless I'm going to have to carry all of them.

Various manufacturers are bringing out bags specifically for this purpose now. They look fine. Al Wind, noted guide on the Green River and other points from the Florida flats to New Zealand, inspired me to the idea with a camera bag that held a formidable amount of gear and was also formidably organized. It's been a settling idea; I've gone through nightmares in the past trying to decide what to carry and what to leave home. Now all that I might need sort of floats along with me in my boat bag, and I can make my choices much nearer to the situation that asks for a decision.

Inventory of the author's boat bag:
Dry, wet, streamer, nymph, and special lake fly boxes. Pocket camera and film. Sunscreen. Fingerless gloves. Spare spool for light rod. Shooting-head wallet. Minibinoculars. Pliers. Leaders. Gary Borger's Color System pamphlet. Mini-fly-tying kit. Swiss army knife.

CLOTHES FOR STILLWATER FISHING

Whatever you wear for fishing lakes and ponds, it should blend in to a degree with what surrounds it. Bright shirts and white hats look great in photos, but they also startle trout that might discover them abruptly. But I think "abruptly" is the key word: It's movement more than brightness that starts trout to fleeing.

When fishing small waters it's best to blend with the surrounding vegetation. Dark shirts and hats are excellent; camouflage would be perfect. On larger waters, especially if you're out in a boat or tube, you're more likely to be seen against the sky than the shoreline. Solid and somewhat light colors such as pale blue or tan are best then.

Your hat should have a wide brim to keep the sun out of your eyes, improving your vision. It also keeps sun off your nose and ears, which, with sunscreen, will keep you from glowing like Rudolph.

I fish a lot of mosquito country, and I believe that one of the best fishing tools to flap down the road in a long time is the long-sleeved canvas shirt. The pesky devils can't poke their needle noses through the hard material. You can roll up long sleeves; a short-sleeved shirt often lets mosquitoes play in the pastures of your forearms.

You need to wear clothes warm enough for the weather you're fishing. I don't have to tell you about that; you can figure it out for yourself. Use the layering system, and be sure you have enough layers if the weather is cool. It's always colder on the water than it is over land. If the weather decides to snort, you'll need a slicker and rainpants.

5

Aquatic Transportation

Whatever you propel around a lake becomes an extension of your fishing gear. Whether it's a float tube, pram, cartopper, canoe, or a bass boat that glides along with a trolling motor, your transportation becomes the launching platform for your cast and is therefore an extremely important part of it. Because stillwater trout constantly move, and the edges of lakes are often abrupt and brushy, what you fish *from* often becomes more important than what you fish *with*.

HIP BOOTS AND WADERS

Even without hippers or waders you can often rock-hop or walk the backs of floating logs around the edges of a lake or pond. When hiking dry, though, you're going to be restricted to the few places where shoreline brush stands back and allows you a backcast. Most lakes have a rocky point or two. Some lakes have meadowed flats that hold back the brush. A few lakes even have sandy beaches where a forty- to fifty-foot cast places the fly over fishable water.

One of my favorite lakes has a windward shore rimmed with fallen logs, most of them floating and bleached by the sun. If they're lodged against each other just right, I can hike some of them, get surprised by others, but still cover lots of water without getting my feet wet. There are times, though, when the wind loosens the jackstraw tangle, or even pushes the logs off toward a different shore. Then I'm tempted into taking the kinds of chances that lead to disasters that have splashes as their punctuation points.

If the water is warm, you can wade wet and mince around at least some of the shoreline on almost any lake. But water temperatures reach comfortable wading levels most often in shallow, eutrophic waters, which are the kind most likely to have mucky bottoms that will suck you in up to your knees and remove your shoes when you try to struggle back to shore.

When water temperatures reach a point where it's comfortable to wade wet in typical trout lakes, the trout are not hanging around in shallow water anyway. The thermocline has already settled itself, and trout have usually moved out toward the cooler depths.

In my experience the water you can reach while fishing dry is severely limited in most lakes and ponds. It's frustrating to fish without some way to get out from shore.

Hip boots will often get you through swampy margins that surround the edges of some stillwaters, delivering you to a firmer bottom that you can stand on and from which you can fish. I have a favorite pond that requires trudging through a bunchgrass swamp for a couple hundred yards before the shore is reached. Hip boots are perfect for getting me there. When I arrive, they are perfect for standing on top of the half-submerged bunchgrass clumps from which I do most of my casting. They also get me out on an occasional log that's awash but forms a fine platform when I'm wearing boots.

Hip boots will get you out deep enough to fish many lakes where the shoreline is sloped and the bottom rocky or sandy. But you have to be careful. It's easy to get fooled by a soft spot and get mired, or to go in over the tops. If you've ever left a hip boot stuck in the bottom ooze, you'll know precisely what I mean.

Not many shorelines are shaped right for wading in hip boots,

The wadered angler can often cover a lot of the best water, even on a vast lake. Trout spend lots of time in the shallows, especially at those times of year when fishing is best.

but a surprising number can be fished wearing chest-high waders if you use some caution.

Waders are far more useful than hip boots, although sometimes less comfortable, especially in hot weather when they tend to cook you when you're not in the water. But they're worth it. In lakes with firm bottoms and gently sloping shorelines you can often get out far enough from the brushline to cover lots of water.

My father and I fought campground bears for the privilege of fishing a couple of remote lakes in the Oregon Cascades one spring. We used prams for two days before discovering that we could wade the edges and present our flies just fine in the kind of shallow water that held fish at that time of year, and with lots less disturbance. The trout were boat shy. By wading slowly on the silty but compact bottom we were able to cover some weed edges and take more trout because we could cast shorter and present our flies more gently.

I discovered something while wading that I've managed to apply to float tubing and boat fishing in the years since. It's simply this: By getting in close to shore, as you have to do while wading, you cast *out* into the lake and retrieve *in* toward shore. Trout respond better to many types of nymphs and streamers when they're fished in this direction. It's true especially for damselfly dressings and for Olive Woolly Buggers with most of their tails pinched off, which is what I use most often now to imitate large dragonfly nymphs.

It's interesting that both of these food forms migrate toward shore to crawl out for emergence. Perhaps trout are accustomed to seeing them hiking toward the edge, not away from it, and respond better to a fly retrieved in the right direction. Whatever the reason, I've found that by wading and casting out into the lake I often take more trout than I do by parking offshore in a pram or tube, casting in and retrieving the fly out toward deeper water.

You have to let these kinds of lessons carry over into all of your fishing. Now I often take my tube or pram right up against the bank, park there, and cast parallel to the shore or out away from it into the lake. It seems foolish to fight bankside brush when you could easily move farther out and cast without hindrance. Still, I find this method effective, and I often lose more flies to trees when fishing a lake in springtime shallows than I do while fishing a tiny stream hemmed in by alders.

There are definite limits to waders. Mucky bottoms rule them out right away. Tall rushes and reeds along the shoreline and mats of floating plants make it tough to wade and cover any water. Such plants take to soft bottoms, so you're not likely to be able to wade well where they grow well. Forested banks tight behind any shoreline make it tough to fish anything but a short cast. Sometimes you're limited to a roll cast unless you can wade farther out from shore.

Shores that drop off steeply into deep water obviously limit your range when you fish in waders. Some lakes and ponds, because they angle down so fast from banks that are massed with trees behind, don't allow you to fish an inch of shoreline when you wear waders.

You have to have some way to get farther out from shore.

FLOAT TUBES

Tony Robnett and I motored in a cartopper to the upper end of a lake in the Kamloops region of Canada. When we got to where we wanted to fish, we beached the boat, tossed float tubes over the edge, slipped cautiously into them, and flippered away.

A man restricted to the shore nearby watched it all happening. His voice, rich with a Scottish accent, rolled across the still lake toward us. "That's a fine bit of frumpery you've got there," he said.

Tony and I considered our tubes fine bits of freedom.

When fishing from a tube you have a few freedoms that you don't have even when fishing from a boat, although you also have some new restrictions to live with. Tubes leave your hands free from duty at the oars, so they can tend at all times to your cast and retrieve. You can position yourself constantly with a mere flick of a flipper without ever setting the rod down.

A float tube might be the single best investment you could make in a new piece of lake fishing gear.

A tube allows you to poke along a shoreline or the edge of a drop-off, casting and retrieving without interruption and without disturbing the water or banging the boat. You can move into position over a weed bed, or just off its edge, and hover there without drifting out of position. With a tube you can troll or wind-drift pleasantly without letting go of your rod, the advantages of which become evident when you get a strike and can strike back without having to reach for the dancing rod.

Float tubes are excellent for exploring a body of water that is reasonably small, thirty acres or less. They're perfect on the kind of water where you can't launch a boat. But as Tony and I know, they also have advantages on water where it's no problem to insert a cartop boat.

If you're going to make a single investment for fly-fishing lakes, I would suggest that it be in a float tube. A tube costs less than a new fly rod. If you're dissatisfied with the rod you own for lake fly-fishing, buy a tube rather than a new rod, and you'll see that this fine bit of frumpery makes your old rod fish a lot better.

Types of Float Tubes

Float tubes come with or without truck-tire inner tubes. Those without have an airtight skin and almost always have two air chambers for safety. They are light, can be carried compacted, and can be blown up at the lake with lung pressure. That makes them great when you have to hike more than a mile or so to reach a lake. You can carry an inflated tube of the regular sort that far if you rest a bit along the way. Use a tumpline type of carry: Rest the rim of the tube on your head and you'll find that it's surprisingly light.

Lightweight float tubes are at their best for short backpacking trips – overnight or weekend stays where you don't have to pack a lot of food and camping gear in addition to the tube. The reason is evident when you stack up the accessories – waders and flippers – that accompany a tube. Add that to your normal backpacking gear and you're going to have a heavy pack for a long trek.

The regular sort of float tube, with a truck inner tube, has the advantage of floating you higher in the water, which makes a terrific difference when tubing. Float tubes with inner tubes inside are naturally heavier. They must be inflated at a service station, or before you leave your car, using an electric pump. A hand pump delivers so little volume that you will strain away for a long time before getting much rise out of something the size of a float tube. Most regular tubes have a smaller car or wheelbarrow tube inside a backrest, providing both comfort and safety. If your truck tire should get punctured—a remote chance—you'd still have transportation to shore, although you'd become thoroughly wet getting there. But tubes are under so little pressure that even a large leak gives you time to hustle like a duckling toward shore.

Blowouts seem an alarming possibility to beginning tubers. But they don't happen on the water. If anything blows out, it will be the stitching in the canvas around the tube, and that will happen only if the tube is overinflated. So it's going to happen at a service station, not on the water. It can also happen in the back of your car or pickup if you blow your tube up tight, then take a road that gains several thousand feet of elevation on your way to the lake. You have to figure on elevation gains and leave your tube slightly soft if you're going tubing in the mountains.

You'll also want to avoid leaving your tube sitting in the hot sun while you're grounded for lunch or a snooze. The air inside will expand and strain the stitching. Leave the tube sitting in the water, which is cooler than the air. This keeps expansion down, and you won't have a problem.

Whichever kind of tube you use, be sure that it comes with a casting apron. A tube without a place to lay your line during the retrieve is worthless, especially when you cast a sinking line. As you retrieve, the line will drop down inside the tube, sink, and tangle with your flippers. If you get it wrapped around a leg, you'll have to go all the way to shore to disentangle yourself.

Gearing Up for Tubing

You need to wear chest waders to use a float tube in most trout waters. In spring and fall neoprenes are best because of their extra insulation. Lightweights are fine in summer with a set of pile pants under them if the water is still somewhat cold; with a pair of sweatpants if it's warm enough. Since the surface layers of a lake absorb the most warmth from the sun, it's surprising the length of the season that you can get away with wearing lightweight waders. But don't stretch that season. You're in almost total contact with the water from the time you insert yourself into a tube. Your body temperature will get lowered if you don't dress right, and you'll get driven to shore shivering even on a warm, sunny day. Avoid wearing denim jeans under waders when tubing. They'll chafe you behind the knees, sometimes wearing the skin raw.

Always use swim fins. Some special flippers fit on your heels and let you push yourself forward. But that's not the way you want to go when you're positioning yourself for fishing. And forward is not where you'll want to go when you hook a hot fish. It's best to be able to back up, which is what swim fins enable you to do. When you want to make time, turn around and flipper along backward.

Lately I've been using fins that go on over wading shoes. A couple of times I've let the wind take me far downlake, then I've gotten out, removed the flippers, and hiked back to where I got in. Of course, you can always use regular swim fins over stocking-foot waders and tie a pair of tennis shoes to the back of the tube. When you exit the lake far from your origins, take off the fins and waders, tie on the shoes, and stride off. It's easy. But it's impossible if you don't have some sort of shoes along. Always take them unless you're on a very small lake and know that you're going to have no trouble getting back to where you started.

Always pare your gear to the essentials when tubing and wear a short vest. Long vests dangle their lower edges and pockets in the water even in the best of tubes. You'll have wet cameras, fly boxes, toilet paper, and whatever else you tend to carry in bottom pockets. Even with a short vest it's best to put cameras and other undunkables in the pockets of the tube itself to insure that they'll stay dry. Sometimes I'll take just the few things that I need—fly boxes, tippets, nippers—in the pockets of the tube and leave the vest at the rig.

A landing net is not a luxury when fishing from a float tube. If you ever get a large trout flapping around and leading you in circles while you try to hand-land it, you'll know what I mean. A net lets you subdue the fish in an orderly fashion, which means you can release it in good health, not worn out.

A portable electric inflator is almost an essential if you do a lot of tubing. It lets you store the tube empty at home and drive to the lake with the tube tucked in a corner, taking up little room. Set the pump to perking by plugging it into the cigarette lighter. Keep an occasional eye on it while you get your waders on, your gear pared down, and yourself ready for tubing. Electric pumps tend to overheat, and they need to be rested at times to cool off, especially on hot days.

Inserting Yourself

Once you're geared up and the tube is inflated, it's time to get launched upon the waters. If you've never tubed before, you're in for some surprises. The first is how quickly you acquire a sense of security when dangled from the straps of your tube. But first you have to get all of your weight suspended from it. To do that you have to launch backward.

Step gingerly into the tube on shore. Getting your fins into the tube and past the suspension system is one of the most difficult operations because of all the awkwardness. Once you're in, and still standing, make sure all of the buckles and straps are securely latched. You don't want the surprise of shooting out the bottom as soon as you sit down.

Once everything is secure, hoist the tube around your waist, take aim, and head for the water in reverse while watching over your shoulder. A gently sloping, firm shoreline is a real help here. Don't try launching for the first time in mud.

Walk backward, to keep from stubbing your flippers, right to the water and on out into it. When the tube rises up and floats you away, you'll feel insecure for about ten seconds. Sit back and relax and you'll be amazed at how soon you feel like you've been doing it forever.

Because of your low center of gravity and absolute flotation, you're probably safer during a storm than you would be in a small boat. You might not be as comfortable, though, and the wind is going to have its way with you. But you won't tip over or be tossed out. There have been cases when tubers survived storms that boaters didn't.

When you're finished fishing, you remove yourself from the water the same way you entered it: backward. Paddle toward shore until you can stand up. Lift your tube up around your waist with both hands, then step out of the water. Watch carefully over your shoulder to make sure you don't run into anything. When you're aground, drop the tube and step carefully out. Again, this is when you can get tangled up easily and have an embarrassing fall.

Advantages and Disadvantages

The advantages of a tube lie mostly in the freedoms I've mentioned. They leave your hands free for fishing. They are light to carry and take up a lot less storage room than a boat. You can get them into places you could not take a boat. They are safe, fun, and quiet in surroundings that often seem assailed by the sounds of a motor or even the banging of a boat. They give you a low profile and seem to disturb fish far less than a boat, although on calm water you have to move smoothly to keep waves to a minimum.

The disadvantages are serious. You draw lots more water, three to four feet of it as opposed to three to four inches in a boat. You're in such close contact with the water that, if it's very cold, as it is in early spring when fishing can be great, tubing is a short-duration activity even when wearing neoprenes. Your range is limited. You can't cover water nearly as fast, or roam as far, as you can in a boat, even a rowboat.

Wind is a problem. A breeze doesn't do much, but a high wind, as lakes often seem to suffer, will cause you to struggle in order to maintain position. Still, you have to fight that in a boat, too, and you need your hands, not your feet, to do it. The main thing to watch with wind is not getting pushed out from shore on a huge lake, one you wouldn't want to cross. And don't go too far with the wind if your only way to get back is by water. You might find yourself in for a long, tedious paddle.

And, you have to visit shore to tinkle.

PRAMS, CARTOPPERS, AND CANOES

I'm a fan of prams. I appreciate their lightness, quickness, and the fact that I can stand up and cast in them, which is difficult to do in a float tube. My pram is plywood, just under eight feet long, wide in the stern, too narrow in the bow to offer much flotation, and too

A pram is the author's favorite aquatic transportation, although this one, called the *Barkchip*, is slightly cranky.

low in freeboard to be safe on any sort of rough water, although it got its name on the brawling Deschutes River.

I was floating alongside Richard Bunse, who had all of my valuables stored in his sixteen-foot drift boat. We bounced through a rapid. Bunse looked over in the middle of it and shouted, "You look like a frog sitting on a chip of bark." Ever since, I've called my pram the *Barkchip*. I've tried to get rid of it several times, because of all its defects, but it keeps coming back to me, and I keep liking it.

Prams can be carried in a small pickup or tossed onto the top of a car. They are easy to get to the water and they don't require a launching ramp. If the road and the lake don't quite get together, you can drag a pram a few hundred yards when you have to.

Cartoppers are similar, but they are usually enough bigger that they can hold two people instead of one and sometimes can take a motor. Most cartoppers are aluminum to save weight, which means they make a lot of noise, which I don't like. Perhaps that's one reason I prefer to fish from a float tube or a pram. But cartoppers are ideal for lakes larger than fifty acres, and there are things you can do to quell their noise.

Canoes, of course, are long, pointy, and tippy. They are classic fly-fishing boats, but you have to have good balance and smooth water to fish out of them standing up. It's not very convenient to fly-fish sitting down, and the view is better when you stand. Wind-drift is a pain in a canoe; you have to set your rod down, pick up the paddle, and use both hands to move back into the position you want. Canoes don't anchor easily because of their shape. Unless you anchor both ends they tend to skitter around in the wind.

But canoes are beautiful, and they'll glide through narrow connecting waterways and reed channels with ease. Some lakes, especially forested lowland lakes or pristine high-mountain lakes, cry out for the quiet and grace of a canoe. I love canoes in their place, but I'd far rather fish out of a blunt-nosed and ugly pram.

A canoe is classic fly-fishing transportation. *Jim Schollmeyer*

Outfitting a Pram or Cartopper

Quiet and simplicity are the keys. Everything that goes into a fly-fishing boat should serve one of those two goals. The oars and oarlocks should be quiet. Your anchor setup, which is one of the things you need since you want to be able to stay on station at times, should be quiet. The *Barkchip's* anchor rope goes out over a pulley at the bow. If I lower it slowly, it doesn't make any noise.

You don't want to toss your anchor over the side with a splash. If you do, it will be time to move on before it ever reaches bottom.

You need a bailing sponge, life jacket, and landing net when fishing from a pram or small boat. Beyond that, keep clutter to a minimum. When I first got the *Barkchip*, I went over it and removed all fittings, cleats, screw eyes, and anything else that could catch a fly line. I fish out of the stern end. Everything I need for the day—lunch, boat bag, cameras, rain gear—goes in the bow where it's out of the way.

I recently discovered a giant Rubbermaid plastic box with lid that all of the guides are using on whitewater trips. It holds a mountain of gear, keeps it out of any water that gathers on the bottom, and has a watertight lid to keep out spray and splash. Best of all, it holds everything and quells the stew that sometimes gets to stirring around in the bottom of a boat, snagging fly lines. The only things left to catch it are my two feet.

One day I fished with Jerry Bliss, of the Sespe Fly Fishers in California. He put this thing about feet alarmingly well: "If I had only one leg, I'd still stand on my fly line!" Wear shoes with smooth soles, not wafflestompers.

Advantages and Disadvantages

You get a higher platform when you stand to cast from a pram, a cartopper, or, if you dare, a canoe. It helps to see what's going on, and also helps to make casting easier since you have the full range of arm and body motion. You have a lot longer traveling range than you do in a float tube and can cover a larger lake, following fish movements or scouting to find them. You can carry a wider range of options, including your full boat bag. You can also fish with a couple of rods rigged constantly if you'd like to.

There are disadvantages. When you stand up, trout can see you better than they can when you're dangled from a tube. To position the craft you have to sit down, set your rod aside, and take up the oars. That's when you'll get a strike. A boat will swing on the anchor rope in the wind; you can't keep your position with your feet. A boat is noisier than a float tube.

The logistics of owning and storing a boat are difficult if you live in an apartment. A tube will go in a closet; most boats won't.

TRAILERABLE BOATS

Large bodies of water call for large boats unless you want to be restricted to nibbling at their edges. Most of us are content with that, and there are good reasons for it. Trout, when they are in water that is favorable to fly-fishing, are caught in association with the shoreline most of the time. A float tube, pram, canoe, or cartopper will get you out to them without trouble or danger.

But you might find times when you want to fish the pelagic regions of a large lake, and a big boat is the only safe way to do it.

There are other reasons for large boats. All of the electronic wizardry used in bass fishing can also help you find trout in lakes. A fishfinder is an obvious advantage when trout are suspended down near the thermocline. I can't say that my own experience extends to that kind of fishing, with those kinds of advantages. Most often when trout are deep, I gather what clues I can assemble, then dangle a fly deep behind a float tube or pram and paddle slowly away.

But I've had a chance to fly-fish for trout out of somebody else's well-equipped bass boat. I'll have to confess, it has lots of advantages. You couldn't find a better casting platform than the bow and stern decks of a bass boat. It's also the ultimate for fishing range, although you'll have to accept some disturbing roar to get where you're going. It's hard to imagine a quieter or more efficient way to move into position and hold yourself there than with a trolling motor. With proper carpeting a bass boat is almost as quiet as a float tube.

You can even take a nap in a bass boat.

There are some disadvantages. Cost is a large one. A nicely rigged boat will start at around $6,000 and go up from there. Maintenance is another. A bass boat is not an airplane, but it takes a lot more care and feeding than a float tube or pram. It requires far too much for an unmechanical soul like me. I would consider myself burdened if somebody gave one to me.

Bass boats tend to be cluttered with cleats and ropes, pedals and handles, wires and tubes and throttles. Much of this can be subdued with a fine mesh netting spread over the top to keep the fly line free.

You're restricted to places with boat ramps.

Most trailerable boats are set up for something besides fly-

It's difficult to beat the convenience of a bass boat's casting platform, if you don't mind the logistics of owning the boat.

fishing. If you acquire one and want to convert it, start by removing everything you possibly can that could catch a fly line. Strip the platforms of cleats, seats, cables, wires, and whatever. If there are gaps that let the line fall down among batteries and gas tanks, cover the gaps with netting. If the boat has exposed aluminum surfaces, carpet them. You can see that it begins to get complicated.

But it's often worth it.

6

The Three Major Variables

I had a theory. I knew the lake was full of leeches and large trout. I figured a black Marabou Muddler fished deep with a patient retrieve would look just like an ugly leech undulating along the bottom, looking for something innocent to eat.

I strung my rod with a sinking line and tied the Marabou to a stout 3-foot tippet. I waded waist-deep into the spring-chilled water, then flung out a long cast. While the line tugged the fly down I gazed around at the sagebrush hills and high mountains surrounding the Oregon desert lake. Then I drew my attention in from the hills and began a slow, teasing retrieve.

It was time to test my theory.

After about ten feet I felt a sullen tug. I reared back to set the hook, and let out a shout to Tony Robnett, fishing just down the line. The trout yanked back hard, took a two-foot surge, then stubbornly refused to budge. I rapped it with the rod again, knowing I was into a big one, thankful for the strength of that short leader.

Tony reeled up and rushed over to watch the fight. The fish

stayed where it was but began to shake its head violently against the pressure of the raised rod. I tipped the rod over to the side, a trick I had learned from fighting steelhead. It upsets fish and makes them move.

It didn't work with this one, however. It stayed right where it was. I tugged, and the fish tugged back. This went on for about five minutes before Tony quietly coughed into his hand and said, "Hey, Davie, I think you've caught yourself a submerged sagebrush."

Simpleminded statements like that always hurt the most when they're true.

I broke off, tied on a new fly, and cast again. I caught another sagebrush top. The fight was quicker and a lot quieter, but the outcome was just the same. And like most fools with half-baked theories, I had been overconfident when I left the rig and had not brought a floating line.

One thing I've learned about lake fishing is that you can't fish ten feet deep in five feet of water.

I decided to get some casting practice if nothing else. So I walloped out a long cast and instantly stripped the fly back as fast as I could make it go, racing it above the sage tops. The Marabou Muddler was so shallow that it left a slight wake. I wasn't half through the first retrieve when another wake welled up behind it, arrowed in on it, and ended in a bold boil punctuated by a violent rap on my rod.

Tony didn't pay any attention to my shouts this time, but he did when a 4-pound trout hung heavy in the bottom of my net.

That first trout was an accident, but the two that followed it were not. Soon Tony and I were both wading at the edge of the lake, casting long, retrieving fast, and catching fat trout.

I've learned since that day that it's rarely an accident when you change something dramatically and suddenly start catching trout. What you have to find when you fish lakes and ponds for trout is that combination of things that the trout will accept. Until you find it, you're likely to catch more sage tops than trout. Once you find it, the trout suddenly seem easy.

The problem of finding what the trout want sometimes seems overwhelming. But it's actually simple, because there are just three factors to work with: fly type, depth fished, and speed of retrieve. Once these three things get lined up in sympathy with what the trout want, you have it made and the trout are in trouble, no matter where you fish stillwaters, anywhere in the world.

FLY TYPE

The type of fly that you select should be based on what trout are accustomed to eating. In a lake barren of leeches I'd have wasted time tossing the black and ugly Marabou Muddler. In a lake full of leeches and little else I'd have had a tough time interesting a 4-pound trout in a #16 midge. Of course, the opposite is also true: In a lake with a major population of midges, small flies will interest the largest trout.

One way to discover the common grocery in a lake is simply by asking around. Check at resorts, tackle shops, or wherever fishermen gather. Snoop around campgrounds and boat landings. When you see somebody with a nice fish and you show a modest amount of interest, you'll have to gag him to keep him from telling you every detail about how he caught it. If the fish hasn't been cleaned, you can make yourself a hero and find out a lot of the news you need by offering to do the chore.

If you can't find out what fish are taking by asking around, then you can find out by looking around, observing what is on and in the water. The most common fish foods in lakes can be broken down into three categories: aquatic insects, crustaceans, and other critters.

The aquatic insects most important in stillwaters include mayflies and midges, caddisflies, damselflies, and dragonflies. Activity of these insects in the air is an indication that trout will be feeding on them at one time or another during the course of a day. But it also indicates something that might be more important as you seek a strategy for fly selection: It tells you that the nymphal and larval stages of these insects are active under the water where you can't see them. Do some poking around with an aquarium net or a kitchen strainer, or by pulling up weeds to see what wiggles out of them.

What you want to discover is the predominant food form in the water you're about to fish. That's what fish are most likely to be seeing and feeding on. It's what you want to base your fly selection on unless some specific stage of a particular insect has their attention riveted. If that's happening, you want to know about it, too,

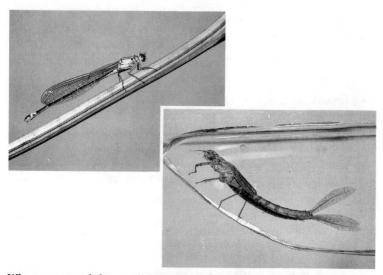

When you see adult aquatic insects nearby, such as this damselfly, it might be an indication that nymphs of the same insect are active under the water and becoming part of the diet of trout.

and select your fly pattern based on what's happening at the moment.

Crustaceans in lakes are often the predominant food form. The group includes large and visible crayfish. But smaller scuds are usually more important, simply because in water that makes them happy they exist in astonishing numbers. They are awkward beasts that tumble about in and around weed beds and shoreline vegetation. Even the largest trout key on them because of their abundance at times when other food forms are not active.

The other critters mentioned are usually either leeches or baitfish. Discovering the presence of these can be difficult, sometimes requiring the catching of that magical first fish for dinner and a stomach sample. But most trout are too valuable to kill; certainly you wouldn't want to kill one simply to see what it has been eating. There are other ways to discover the presence of these big bites.

Leeches will come running if you crack open an egg and set it in the shallows at night. Use a flashlight, and it will reveal a world to you that you might find fascinating, beyond its value to you as a fisher of flies.

Selecting a fly pattern to represent the predominant food form is of such major importance that it is the subject of Part 3, Lake Food Forms and Their Imitations. Briefly, if fish feed on smaller forms—mayfly nymphs, caddis larvae, or scuds—a general suggestive pattern such as a Zug Bug or Gold-Ribbed Hare's Ear in #12 to #14 will usually resemble them closely enough to interest trout. If fish are selective and ignore these offerings, change to a dressing that more closely resembles the real thing.

If fish feed on larger insects, such as dragonfly and damselfly nymphs, you can fish for them with dressings such as Olive Woolly Worms and bushy Carey Specials. I've recently been bobbing the tail of an Olive Woolly Bugger in the appropriate size when I discover dragons or damsels abundant in a lake. You want to use flies that not only resemble the larger insects but also have lots of moving parts to capture the movements of the naturals.

Lakes with populations of leeches and baitfish call for fishing with streamer dressings. Where big fish feed on little fish, traditional featherwing and bucktail dressings such as the Coachman, Mickey Finn, and Little Brook Trout work well. If sinuous leeches live in the lake, nothing beats the movement inherent in marabou patterns such as the Marabou Muddler or Woolly Bugger.

Your fly selection should always be based on what you suspect trout see at some time during the day. If trout feed selectively, you have to find out about it, and you have to match what they've been taking.

DEPTH FISHED

The second factor in a successful stillwater strategy is the depth at which you fish the chosen fly. I had the importance of depth knocked a little deeper into my head one evening recently. I like to row the *Barkchip* around for exercise at times. When trout season is open, I troll a fly while I do it. So I plunked my pram into the shallows at one end of a two-mile-long lake near home. I dangled 50 feet of dry line and a weighted Zug Bug nymph off the stern. Then I headed down the lake.

The wind was at my back, and I whizzed along. The fly stayed up near the surface, and no fish rose to take it. When I got to the far end of the lake, I turned around and headed back toward the rig. The wind was in my face and it slowed me down. I got about one hundred yards before my rod tip snapped down and I dropped the oars to grab awkwardly for it. Too late!

After another fifty yards the rod popped down again. This trout hooked itself, and I lost almost all of my progress into the wind while playing the fish.

I started off again, and again caught a fish before I got very far up the lake. It took three more fish for the lesson to sink in: The boat was going so slow that the weighted nymph was getting down about six feet where fish were feeding.

Trout hold at certain depths, sometimes as stratified as a summer lake, primarily in response to the availability of food. If insects, crustaceans, or baitfish are up near the surface, that is where you are most likely to find trout. And the trout you find there will be actively feeding, so they will be most susceptible to your enticements.

Evidence of surface-feeding fish is easy to gather. You will see the fish or their rises. And it's an easy step from there to determine what they are taking. All you have to do is examine the water closely to see what's on the surface. You base your pattern on that, and the depth fished is right on top.

But it's common for trout to make rise-rings while taking something just beneath the surface. This is a confusing situation because you'll see the rises and try dry flies, but you won't catch any trout. When this happens, try replacing your dry with a nymph or wet fly fished at a depth just a few inches beneath the top.

When trout aren't feeding visibly at all, they can sometimes be found feeding at middepths. Trout might be anywhere between the bottom and the top at times like these, and these are definitely times to try your patience. The trout are hard to find.

Certain conditions cause them to hold at middepths. A hatch of insects might be gearing up down below, but no evidence of it has reached the top yet. Or a migration of insects might be going on, since many mature aquatics pack their bags and head toward shore as nymphs, preparing to crawl out on land and emerge into the aerial adult form. These migrations cause midwater feeding by trout, and you have to respond with a midwater presentation of your fly.

When trout do feed at middepths, there isn't much to tell you about it. There is really only one good way to find out, and that is to change the depth at which you fish until you find where the fish hold.

Trout hold and feed along the bottom a lot more often than they do at middepths, given that the water depth is not beyond the limits of light, and therefore has vegetation growth. The simple reason is the presence of food; most forms spend most of their time on or near the bottom. Weed beds are located down there. So are most of the terrestrial leaves that fall into a lake or pond. All of this becomes fuel for insects, and the insects become fuel for trout. The bottom is where trout do their foraging if no specific insect or other activity draws them upward.

You can use a weighted fly to fish at various depths, as I did the day I went rowing for exercise. But it's not the only way, or even the best way. It's better to select the proper sinking line to get the fly down and use an unweighted fly so it retains a lively action.

I've already discussed the ways to achieve depth: a series of wet-tip, wet-belly, and wet-head lines, a range of sinking lines with varying sink rates, or a shooting-head system. Whatever system you choose, be sure it allows you to explore all the depths you're likely to encounter on the water you want to fish.

SPEED OF RETRIEVE

Speed of retrieve should be based to a large extent on the movement of the natural food your chosen fly imitates. If you use a pattern that looks like a cased caddis larva, it would be unwise to retrieve it fast because a caddis larva rarely gallops. If you imitate a leech, you should wallop your fly along at times, because they can undoubtedly sense when a trout is after them, and they swim fast when it happens. At other times leeches creep along the bottom, in sightless search for prey, and you want to fish your imitation slowly.

Some elemental retrieves include the hand-twist, a slow stripping retrieve, a combination of stripping with the line hand while twitching the fly along with the rod tip, a fast strip, and a swift retrieve in which you take the line in with long pulls as fast as you can make them. These retrieves cover most stillwater situations and mimic the movements of most trout food forms. They'll be covered in more detail in the following chapters on stillwater strategies.

CHANGE AS A STILLWATER STRATEGY

I've ceased to consider it an accident when I change one of the three factors of stillwater fishing—fly pattern, depth fished, or speed of retrieve—and suddenly start catching trout. Whether the change is prompted by some visible signal, a previous experience, a wild hunch, or nothing at all, changing what you are doing is important if no fish are coming to your fly.

Change itself is an essential element of a successful stillwater strategy.

A lake strategy calls for experimentation with all three factors of success. It is more than possible to have two of them right and one of them wrong and still not catch any trout: It's the most likely outcome. But base your choices on what's around you, and you're likely to get the three factors right without recourse to hunch and hope.

7

The Dry Fly and Reluctant Trout

The pond was lifeless; not a trout rose. The banks were closed in so tight with alders that Dad rigged a spinning rod and bubble, choosing the heresy of casting his flies with that rather than fighting the brush with a fly rod. I didn't own a spinning outfit, so I found a floating log to wobble out on. After some near adventures I arrived gingerly at a place where I could get a backcast and lay out a forecast if I didn't fire hard enough for the recoil to knock me off the log.

The water was shallow, four to six feet deep alongshore and around the log, and about ten feet deep out toward the center. It didn't look like the trout would come up, so I strung my rod with a wet-tip line and tied on a nymph to get my offering down a few feet.

But Dad couldn't fish deep with a spin rod and bubble. He was restricted to fishing just a few inches under, and for some contrary reason chose to fish a dry fly instead of a wet or nymph. It was a #10, some sort of caddis with a deer-hair wing and brush of brown hackle at its head. He didn't even have to dress it with floatant to keep it afloat. He made his first cast, looping the line far out over the undisturbed water. The bubble plunked in, the fly parachuted in behind it, and Dad immediately began his first retrieve.

I settled in for some patient casting and retrieving, which is usually necessary on any midsummer stillwater. While the line tugged my fly down behind it on the first cast, I idly watched the progress of Dad's dry fly; our eyes are always drawn to a fly that is drifting on a current in a stream or scooting across the surface of a stillwater. When something moves we watch it.

Suddenly something began moving behind Dad's fly. It was a wake welling up. I couldn't believe it, but it ended in a minor detonation, some furious reeling, a trout thrashing on shore, and I was forced to consider it. Of course it was an accident, which is what I shouted to Dad, who agreed with me and cast again – and caught another trout.

I fumbled a floating line through the guides of my rod, chose the bushiest Elk Hair Caddis I could find in a fly box, and tied it on. For the first few casts I let it sit, expecting a trout to rise up and rap it. None did. So I crept it over the surface, thinking that some slight movement might entice the trout to the fly. It didn't. Finally I watched Dad, who was still casting his fly out, still beginning to reel it back immediately and without any action added, still catching an occasional trout doing it. I couldn't figure it out.

Things don't always have to make sense in fly-fishing, at least right at first. I made a long cast, let it sit for a few seconds, then began stripping the dry fly in just as I would fish a streamer. A wake built up behind it.

After I'd worn the water out around the only log from which I could cast, and caught a few trout doing it, I tightroped back to shore and nosed through the alders and grasses while Dad continued to fish. Before long I found the caddis that became the inset shot on the cover of *Handbook of Hatches*. It wasn't until I pickled it in alcohol, took it home, and keyed it out to a modest taxonomic level that I discovered it was a traveling sedge.

So that was it, I decided in retrospect: The trout refused any but a moving fly on the surface because they had been feeding on caddis motoring around on top. We hadn't seen it happen; the hatch probably ended just before we arrived at the pond. But the trout had caddis and movement in their memories and were willing to spear toward the top to take skating dry flies.

The traveling sedge can cause active feeding by trout, at times long after the hatch has ended.

Learning from a spin fisherman, even if he's your father, is not the prescribed way to do it. But a fly fisherman has to take his lessons from all sorts of sources if he's going to make any progress at all.

A dry fly is far from the first choice when trout are not rising on a lake or pond. When the water looks lifeless, as it did that day, it's almost always best to try a subsurface fly based on the predominant food form in the stillwater, and then to try fishing it at different levels to find where the fish hold. But a dry will draw trout up in some circumstances, and taking a fish on a dry is enjoyable whenever you can make it happen. So let's look at the times of year, and times of day, when it makes some sense to try a dry fly in the absence of evidence that it will work.

WHEN TO USE THE SEARCHING DRY

Searching the water with a dry can be fruitful whenever trout rise so sporadically and randomly that you can't predict the place of the next rise. This can happen at any time of the season, during any part of the day. You'll see some sign of it when it does: a set of subtle rise-rings here, then a sudden boil a hundred yards over there, followed a few minutes later by another rise in a completely different part of the lake. It's tempting to chase after them. But it's usually best to stay where you are unless one of the trout comes up several times in a restricted area. Then it's worthwhile to stalk them.

Most of the time it's best to let sporadic feeders work their way to you.

Sporadic feeding is a sign of two things. First, the trout are cruising, looking for food. Second, they are taking whatever they happen upon, and they are seldom selective. If your dry fly is out there, sitting placidly on the surface or towed gently across their bows, they'll usually respond to it. But don't get me wrong; they'll also likely respond to a wet, a nymph, or a streamer. There are advantages to fishing those: They allow you to cover more water. Choose the dry in these situations only if you prefer to take your fish on top, or if you get into a rare situation like I did that day with Dad, and the trout demand that you fish on top.

When no trout rise at all, then casting a dry fly is going to be productive only where the fish hold close enough to the surface to notice something up there and have some willingness to rise up and take it. That means shallow water. So the search for times when trout will respond to a searching dry is limited to those times when they are found in shallows.

Spring is the most likely time to fish a searching dry fly. Turn-over stimulates the lake, plant growth takes off, and insects get active; some sprout wings. Trout move into the shallows to take advantage of the sudden abundance of food there. They spend most of their time in water where something landing on top is within their sphere of interest.

In spring the water is warmest from late morning into early afternoon. That is when most hatches happen at that time of year, and it is when trout are most likely to have their attention turned upward. Consequently, the best time to fish drys in spring is mid-day. The worst times are early morning and late evening when it's chilly.

Early summer is also an excellent time to fish drys when the surface is empty of rises. But midday hatches slack off, and trout are most likely to be on the lookout for surface food in the hours just after dawn and before dusk. In late summer, as the hot season progresses, trout move down toward the thermocline and it's often impossible to move them to the top even at morning and evening.

But you have to watch the water temperature then. When it remains below stressful levels for trout, they're quite willing to come up and cruise during windfalls of terrestrials. Again, you will sometimes notice sporadic rises, which can be an indication for a nonimitative dry whenever a specific insect is not present in dominance.

In fall, especially on lakes that stratified in summer but have already turned over, stillwaters enjoy a sudden resurgence of activity. Nutrients get stirred into the shallows. Photosynthesis takes off again and charges the water with oxygen. Trout respond by moving into territory where they'll respond to a dry. Although it would be anthropomorphic to say they're eager to put on weight for winter, still they do feed with an anxiety in fall that makes them gullible at times, possible to fool on flies that would frighten them earlier in the year. But don't depend on this; they're selective if a hatch comes off, and you have to match it, which is the subject of the next chapter.

In winter it's rare for trout to respond to the nonimitative dry fly. If they move into shallows, it's usually in response to an abundance of a particular insect. You should match it. If no insects are active, which is most of the time, then the trout are in deeper water and have no interest in flies presented on top. You'll usually be wasting your time unless you go down after them.

WHERE TO FISH THE SEARCHING DRY

Trout rarely hold near the surface in what I have called the pelagial zone, out far from shore, unless it is in response to a particular food form, usually midges. Yet they have to be near the surface if they're going to respond to a dry fly. That eliminates most of the water not in association with the shoreline.

The searching dry fly is most effective when fished over water from two to six feet deep. Much beyond that and trout are going to be reluctant to come all the way to the top, although it can happen. That means most of your dry-fly fishing in nonfeeding situations should be restricted to coves, sloping shorelines, and the edges of shelves where shallow water takes a sudden dive toward the depths.

You can also draw trout up at times from any weed bed that is

The Adams and Elk Hair Caddis are good examples of searching drys for fishing lakes and ponds. *Jim Schollmeyer*

visible on the surface, even if it's only as a shadowy dark patch. Shoals that reach up toward the top out in open water will also be productive. Even steep shorelines produce for the searching dry as long as you remember to fish up tight against them, not ten to twenty feet out.

FLIES TO USE AS SEARCHING DRYS

I don't want to be specific about dry flies to use when hatches aren't happening, because you probably have your favorites and that's what you should use. The main thing, beyond a buggy and lifelike look, is confidence, and only you can bring that to a fly.

It's hard to go wrong with such productive dressings as the Adams and Elk Hair Caddis. The Adams has the advantage of a bristling smoke of hackle: the mixing of brown and grizzly that gives the fly the appearance of movement even when it's sitting still. It has the posture and upright perch of a mayfly on the water, which adds to its attraction. It also resembles many midges and other insects. It is said that the fly was originally an imitation of a flying caddis with its wings awhir.

The Adams looks like a lot of things.

The Elk Hair is more specifically imitative of caddis. But it also has the advantage of excellent flotation. You can draw it across the water and it won't sink if it's well dressed. If it's not treated with floatant, you can pop it under the water and retrieve it wet. That's not the province of this chapter, but it is an excellent way to catch stillwater trout, which is the subject of this book.

Lots of other flies work just as well. When selecting a fly that will be fished without movement, color is important. The fly should be subdued, in keeping with the natural colors of nature's insects. A fly to be skated across the water attracts trout by motion, and color is less important. But a bright fly will often turn trout away at the last instant. It is wise to have a drab one, such as the Deer Hair Caddis, available for such situations.

Size is less a factor than it is when you must match a hatch. Trout will often spring on something as large as a #6 when they're feeding nonselectively. Most of the time you'll be better off with flies in the range between #10 and #14. At times it's wise to go down to #16, but that's getting into the range of hatch-matching stuff.

METHODS FOR THE SEARCHING DRY

Methods for fishing dry flies when trout aren't rising can be seen as a sequence. It's truly simple and needs no elaboration.

First, try casting the fly out and letting it sit. That's the primary method and the one you'll want to use most of the time. Pop it onto the water over any likely cover – next to shore, above a submerged boulder or log, over a weed bed, alongside a reed forest or lily pad flat. If the water is featureless, cover it in a disciplined pattern, first with an arc of twenty-foot casts, then thirty, and so on out to the ends of your abilities. Be patient; let each cast sit for at least a minute, more if you can handle it.

The biggest problem that I have with fishing the dry fly this way – letting it sit on top of a lifeless lake – is my own inattention. If I do not have high expectations for a rise, or if an expected rise does not arrive within a minute or so of the moment the fly touches down to the water, my mind and eyes begin to wander. That's all right; there are lots of things to see and appreciate on and around any stillwater. But it's best to combine the wandering eye with some other method, such as the retrieved wet, nymph, or streamer, where feel, not sight, keeps you in touch with what's happening to the fly.

I don't know how many times my eye has been drawn down

out of the sky or trees to some disturbance on the water, only to discover that my fly was at the center of it. I rarely get the hook set when that happens; the fish has already spit it out and gone on.

If you get no action within a reasonable time on a fly without movement, give the fly a twitch or two. Don't hurry into this. A twitch can attract the attention of a fish that hasn't seen the fly. And it can trigger a strike from a trout that hasn't made up its mind. But it can also turn away a trout that was just arrowing in for a strike on the still fly. Give the trout a chance to take the fly sitting before you show it any movement at all.

If you get no action after a couple of twitches, try a retrieve of intermittent movement and long pauses. Skate the fly a foot or so, then let it sit. Again, try to be patient. Even though it's movement that draws the trout to the fly, the fish is most likely to take during the times when the fly is not moving.

When no trout respond to the intermittent retrieve, then try skating the fly across the water with long strides. Draw line in with your line hand and raise the rod from water level to almost straight overhead. Skitter the fly slowly, but be sure it leaves a visible wake behind it. Don't stop. If fish demand the fly with movement, it's usually because they've been taking insects that keep chugging until they reach shore. Trout will turn away if the fly suddenly puts on its brakes.

Another method that works well, where conditions are right for it, is the dead-drifted dry fly on the current where an inlet stream enters a pond or lake. Not all stillwaters have substantial inflows. But most do, and you should fish them wherever you find them. Explore them with the dry fly on top before fishing a sunken fly down toward the bottom. It's surprising how often trout will rise to the surface near an inlet. They're used to seeing aquatic insects either drifting down on the current during a hatch or soaring down from the air during an egg-laying flight.

Fish such areas just as you would the stream itself. Drift your fly off to the edges of the current, then over the center, wherever the current is strong enough to give it some movement.

Another method that is effective at times is wind-drifting the dry fly. This works best when the wind is strong enough to make anchoring and casting slightly unpleasant. The water will have a chop on it. You can cast out, let the fly ride the waves, and let your aquatic transportation, boat or tube, drift apace with the fly. Whenever the line draws tight and the fly begins to drag, pick it up and cast again.

Wind-drifting works best over vast shallows, where the fly is always in striking range of fish cruising near the bottom. It also works well over water with intermittent weed beds. You won't be able to spot the individual beds with a wind-riffle on the water. But the fly, drifting along, will cross them from time to time. You'll know when it does cross one: That's where the fish will hit.

I use this method only when I see some evidence that trout are working on the surface, simply because of an impatient personality. If I see an occasional wind-torn rise form, I try wind-drifting a dry. If I don't see rises on a windy day, I'll still use the method, but with a nymph or streamer instead.

Other dry-fly methods slip into the territory of the imitative dry, not the searching dry. It's important to know when to cut your bait with the nonimitative dry. If trout are down and the lake looks lifeless, more often than not you have to go down to them with nymphs or streamers, or put in a lot of fruitless casting time.

The searching dry fly is one of the peripheral methods for fly-fishing stillwaters.

8

The Dry Fly and
Rising Trout

Nunnally Lake is one of a chain of seep lakes in central Washington. They formed in the 1950s when Potholes Reservoir was closed and filled, which forced water into an underground lava aquifer. The water slowly seeped into abandoned channels of Crab Creek, downstream, and filled depressions, which became lakes: cool, clear, plump with plant growth, rich in insect life. Trout thrive there.

The trout are from Kamloops rainbow stock. They're stout and very strong for their size.

I arrived at Nunnally on an early-summer day, expecting to fish down deep with damsel nymphs or scud dressings. But trout rose in pods all around. I inserted myself into my float tube in an awkward hurry, turned my back to the rises, and flippered after them as fast as I could.

Rising trout are a mesmerizing force. I know folks who can drive past a pristine stream or sit by the side of an alpine lake without ever casting a fly, if no trout reveal themselves. But let a single rise-ring appear, even far in the distance, and adrenaline

ignites them. Me, too! When trout get going, it's almost impossible
not to go after them.

When I arrived where the trout had been rising, the disturbance of my arrival pushed them fifty feet farther out. But they
still worked with diligence. It was easy to see what they were
taking; female *Callibaetis* mayflies sprinkled the water, some with
their wings still upright, others with their wings spent. I added a
couple of feet of 5X tippet to a leader that was already 10 feet long.
I tied on a #14 Adams hoping it would be close enough to fool the
fish. It wasn't.

I tried clipping a V-notch out of the bottom hackle fibers. The
fly looked better to me, but it didn't look better to the trout. I
snipped wings and hackle from the top of the fly, which left just a
few fibers sticking out to each side: spent wings lying flush in the
film. That kind of surgery on an Adams is usually sufficient to take
trout whenever *Callibaetis* fall to the water. It didn't.

I finally did what I should have done first: I collected a specimen in my aquarium net. My problem was instantly obvious. The
body of the insect was pale gray on the bottom, almost bordering
on white. And it was a #16, not a #14, which is a mistake I make so
often that I don't know why I fail to automatically account for it.

That brought up a marvelous problem. I could easily clip
down a #16 Adams, but it would still be darker than the natural,
and the trout might still reject it. I had my special box of lake flies
with me, and it contained four dressings that were almost perfect
matches for the natural: split white nutria tails, pale gray fur
bodies, a super grizzly hackle wound several times at the thorax
and clipped along the bottom. The fly had always worked well for
me during *Callibaetis* spinner falls. I had to try it.

The problem was, these flies were tied for a pond near home
where the trout seldom exceed 10 inches long. I had foolishly tied
them on 4X fine-wire hooks.

I had no choice. I clipped the 5X leader back a foot, added
3 feet of 6X tip, and tied one of the fragile flies to it. I placed the fly
gently just to my side of the nearest rise. Nothing happened for a
moment. I was about to lift the fly and cast it to a newer rise, but a
trout rose from nowhere and suddenly thumped it. That's all I felt,
but I knew the trout had felt the barb. I brought the fly in, exam-
ined it, and found what I feared: The point of the hook aimed in

the same direction taken by the tails. A single hit had straightened the hook.

Two hours later I'd had the satisfaction of rising about a dozen of those trout. I'd held two of them in my hands. The largest was about 18 inches long, probably weighed 3 pounds, and took some time to revive because I'd played it so gingerly. The other was slightly smaller, and slightly more vigorous at the end of its battle. Some of the ones I'd lost almost made me weep.

When I finished and the fish quit rising, all four of those fine-wire flies had hooks as straight as pins.

Never, I hope I have now learned, tie flies for lakes on hooks more fragile than 1X fine. A stillwater fly will float when tied on a strong hook. There are very few riffles and rapids on a pond or a lake. Few stillwaters lack the potential to surprise you with a trout that can straighten out a 4X fine-wire hook.

DISCOVERING WHAT TROUT ARE TAKING

It's an illogical first step, but I often fish an old favorite or two if trout are rising and I can't see at a glance exactly what they are taking. The favorite is most often a #14 or #16 Adams, because it has the broadest chance of representing something the trout are willing to take a poke at. It looks like a lot of things that trout eat.

Other favorites vary with the season: perhaps a *Callibaetis* Compara-dun in early spring, a Griffith's Gnat or Mosquito in midsummer, an Elk Hair Caddis or Deer Hair Caddis in the fall. But it doesn't take many refusals to direct me toward the logical first step when fishing a dry fly during a rise – capturing whatever the trout are taking.

What trout might be taking is the subject of Part 3 of this book; I'll cover the methods for discovering it here, and discuss what you might find there. Lake food forms are far too important to discuss as a peripheral part of another chapter. In a large way they are what stillwater fly-fishing is all about. You find what trout are taking, then match it in fly pattern and presentation.

The first way to find out what trout might be taking, assuming that they are rising so you know they are feeding on the surface or very near it, is to lay your rod aside and get your nose down close to the water. This can be an education, and it is a great way to kill some idle time when trout aren't rising. You'll learn a lot in a short time.

Even if the insect you're looking for, the one the trout are taking at the moment, isn't obvious, you'll find the cast shucks of what's been hatching for the last couple of days. It's best to get to the downwind side of the lake for this exercise, if possible, and to find a small cove, floating log, or some other trap that will gather what the wind nudges toward shore.

Be on the lookout for the cast shucks of midges and mayflies. You'll have to look close; they'll be awash right in the film, almost invisible at times. These will tell you about hatches that have happened recently and that are likely to happen again sometime soon during a full day on the lake. If the water is shallow and the sun bright, try to peer down and see if any cast shucks have fallen to the bottom. You won't see any unless they are large. Caddisflies often migrate toward favorite shores, leaving windrows of shucks littering the bottom. You'll also find caddis shucks awash in the film at times.

Examine emergent stalks of bulrush and cattail, lily pads, and anything else sticking out of the water. You might find cast shucks that are evidence of dragonfly or damselfly migrations. You also might find resting adult damsels. This is especially true early and late in the day, if clouds obscure the sun, or whenever the wind blows hard. Damselflies do not fly in wind, or if the sun doesn't shine.

Terrestrials will often find their way into your education when you slow down long enough to peer into the water. Some are so tiny that you have to look a long time before they suddenly spring into your awareness, trapped in the surface film. They might include ants and leafhoppers and beetles. In early summer winged ants make their migrations and find themselves distressed on lakes in great numbers. In fall flying termites emerge from wooded edges and flutter their awkward ways to landings on lakes. Trout know about all these things. You should learn about them, too.

If you can't find a cause for the rises, and they're confined to a narrow area, paddle right into the middle of the rising trout, even if it drives them away. Something might be happening in the restricted area, say over the top of a weed bed, that you need to know about before you can catch anything. If it keeps on happen-

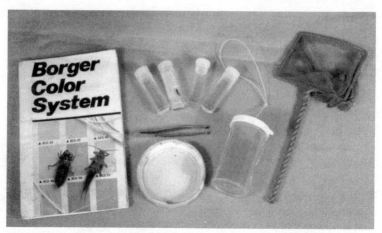

Some basic collecting gear: vials, tweezers, jar lid, rearing cage, aquarium net, and Gary Borger's Color System for color comparisons.

ing, you can back away after you've figured it out, and the trout will return and begin feeding again. It might not be in a hurry, but if you don't gather a handle on what they're taking, it won't matter to you that they keep on rising. All you'll catch is increasing frustration.

Some small items will help you collect what you find on the surface. An aquarium net is perfect for lifting a specimen from the water without damaging it. A small rearing cage, available from fly shops or easy to make yourself out of a pill bottle, will let you view the creature without fear of its escaping. If you don't have a match for the insect in your fly boxes, the same cage will let you take the natural back to your tying table so you can invent your own medicine to match it.

Vials filled with alcohol allow you to pickle the specimen and preserve it for identification. But be aware that the insect will turn to rags as soon as it dies; its shape will need to be remembered. And its color will fade quickly in alcohol. If you can photograph it, that will help. If not, try to note the color and shade of wings and body, with particular attention paid to the belly, not the back.

Lately I've been using Gary Borger's "Borger Color System" pamphlet for a quick reference. I keep it in a Ziploc bag in my boat bag, and it's handy to get an idea what color dubbing will match an insect. James Leisenring, late author of *The Art of Tying the Wet Fly,* insisted on carrying cards with his dubbing materials affixed. When he captured a specimen, he wetted the materials until he found a match. He had two good reasons. First, he wanted to choose his material in the same light where he found trout taking the insect. Second, he knew that dubbing materials darken when wet.

If you use the Borger system, find the color chip in the book that matches the insect. When you sit down to tie, choose a dubbing that matches the color chip after the material has been wetted, not when it's dry. There will be a lot of difference, and trout will approve of your extra effort.

An obvious way to discover what trout are taking, when a specimen evades you in every other way, is to catch a trout and examine its stomach. This works for me only when I want to keep the trout for a meal, which is occasional. I have written elsewhere that I personally do not enjoy invading a trout with a stomach pump or an eviscerating spoon. These things may be all right for you, but not for me. Many of my best friends do it and they are still my friends, although I wag my finger disapprovingly at them when they pry at a trout. They wag theirs just as vigorously at me when I kill a trout.

If you do examine a stomach sample, it helps to have a jar lid, petri dish, or something else to stir it in. Add some water. Work the contents gently so they separate themselves without breaking up. The powerful acids of the trout will already have done great damage to the specimens. But the remaining parts, like pieces of a puzzle, will often tell you what the living picture looked like: a mayfly or caddis, a beetle or an ant.

If a food form is represented by more than two or three specimens, you can be sure trout are aware of it. Matching it will get you some approvals. If only one kind of food is represented in the stomach, you know the trout are feeding selectively and you have to match it or forget it, especially if it's a surface food form.

Selecting a fly to match the insect that you've discovered is the second step in fishing the dry fly over feeding trout.

FLY SELECTION

Trout foods take different forms. But not so many unique forms as one might think. All mayflies have roughly the same shape but vary in size and color. All caddisflies have almost exactly the same shape. The same is true for midges, alderflies, and damselflies. This encompasses the major aquatic insect orders that are important to the stillwater angler as models for dry flies. Terrestrial insects add a few more forms to the equation, but the list is still limited.

Within each order the species vary in size and color. Some orders have a wider range than others. Mayflies vary from Tricos and *Caenis* in #24 or #26 up to Big Yellow Mays, the famous *Hexagenia limbata*, which is a #6 or even #4. Caddisflies, in lake types, are slightly more restricted, ranging from #18 up to #6. Midges might vary from #26 up to #10 during the same season on the same waters. Alderflies, on the other hand, rarely change more than a size or so, from #12 to #10. Damselflies have little variation in size, ranging from #10 to #6.

Colors also run different ranges in the various orders. Alderflies are uniformly blackish brown. Caddis are usually tan, brown, or gray. Damselflies come in tan, red, and the most common blue phase. Midges might be almost any color in the spectrum. Lake mayflies are usually tannish olive, shades of gray, or tannish yellow.

The obvious point is that you can select a pattern style that matches the shape of any of the orders, then vary that style in size and color to match whatever species you encounter. It's a far simpler way to consider fly-pattern selection than the belief that you need a separate dressing for each species. That approach leads to confusion, which is why twenty-five thousand fly patterns have been recorded for American waters.

Don't try to carry that many. Try, instead, to establish a few that work well for you. Then add to the list as you encounter situations that require new dressings. If you've chosen a pattern style for each order of insects, then you can buy or tie variations that match specific hatches. Over time you'll build up a fly box based on the natural foods that trout eat. It will contain only flies that have worked for you over a period of years. Those are the best flies to turn to; you'll have confidence in them.

For me the basic styles are simple, and were recorded in full detail in *Handbook of Hatches*. For the mayflies in stillwater situations I like Compara-duns. For caddis, Elk Hair Caddis work well, although it's often necessary to trim the hackles off the bottom. For midges on the surface I almost always use some form of the Griffith's Gnat. Alderflies, although fully winged and caddislike in shape, sink rapidly when they get on the water and are best imitated with wet flies, not drys. Simple beetle and ant shapes round out the list of pattern styles, upon which the variations are built.

Dry-fly pattern selection should always be based on the size, form, and color of the insect, in that order of importance. You'll be surprised how often you can cobble up a match from something already in your fly boxes using a collected sample as a model and your tippet nippers as a surgical tool.

BEHAVIOR OF THE NATURAL

When collecting an insect try to observe its behavior on the water. This will aid you greatly when trying to decide how to present it.

Most insects will simply sit there, trapped by the film, bewildered about what to do. But not all of them, and not all of the time. For example, a mayfly dun will usually sit patiently, waiting for its wings to dry. But every few seconds it might also test those wings to see if they are ready for flight. If they're not, the result is a slight taxi across the surface, like a seaplane failing to gain takeoff speed.

Lots of insects protest their presence on the water. They kick and struggle and constantly whir their wings. If they are large, this sets up quite a commotion. If they are tiny, it doesn't do much more than set up a high-speed vibration in the surface film. You've noticed it: the tiny sets of wavelets millimeters apart that you can see only if you are inches away or are looking through binoculars. Sometimes you see the disturbance on the water and can't tell what's making it because the insect at its center is so small.

Caddis can go crazy when they get on the surface of a stillwater. Some of the traveling sedges scoot in seemingly aimless circles, although it's likely nature has worked out some aim for them that I have failed to divine. Others motor straight toward shore and don't stop until they get there. Some alternately scoot and sit still.

Alderflies, those luckless ancients, have wings that seem to fail them both in the air and on the water. When they struggle in the surface film, all they manage to do is tear a hole in it, through which they sink.

It's wise to observe as much as you can of insect behavior on

No bit of water is more difficult to fish than a breathless lake, where the slightest disturbance will astonish the trout. *Jim Schollmeyer*

the water, and also in it. You will learn things that direct your presentations. You will learn things that I don't know, since I've not had a chance to watch all the insects that you're going to observe.

PRESENTATION

You've identified the insect that's causing the rises and have chosen a fly to match it. You've noticed the insect's behavior on the water. Now it's time to present the fly so trout believe it's a natural.

The first part of presentation is getting the fly hooked up to the right leader. I discussed leaders in the chapter on tackle, but will repeat here that the purpose of the leader is to turn over at the end of the cast, to separate the fly from the end of the line, and to give the fly some freedom so it floats naturally, not like it's tethered to a rope.

No piece of water is quite as challenging as a breathless lake with trout sipping in its surface. A spring creek flat can be difficult, but it always has a current to deliver your fly to the fish and to mask some of your wading waves. Lakes don't have the kinds of currents that mask your mistakes.

Your leader has to be long, 10 to 15 feet. It must be tapered well enough to turn over and straighten out, as opposed to dying at the end of the cast and landing all in a pile. Yet it must have a tippet that is long and fine so the fly floats freely. It's best if the tippet itself lands with some slack in it: curves, not coils. This is especially critical in a breeze, no matter how light. If the leader lands straight as an arrow, downwind, the fly hangs still when it actually should be moving. This is drag, the same thing that causes problems on streams. Watch for it. Solve it by adjusting your leader or making your casts at a different angle, across or even into the wind. Trout will notice the difference.

Ideally, you want your fly to land lightly, with the leader extended but the tippet slightly serpentined. This is not an easy matter to accomplish. That is one reason lakes reward casting skills. I've pointed out the other reason earlier: The farther you can cast, the more undisturbed water you can cover.

Working a Pod of Fish

Trout in stillwaters often feed in pods when working a hatch. They are not always tightly packed, but they are usually at least loosely associated with each other. Trout move and feed randomly within the pod but drift along with its movements if the pod itself is moving.

The best way to fish a pod of trout is from outside of it, casting toward its edge. You can cover individual trout this way, but your line does not fly through the air over them. You are not as likely to spook two or three of them with each cast. This is not always fatal since others cruise into the area they abandon. But it can eventually get the pod edgy and put the whole thing down. Sometimes that can happen in a cast or two if you are right in the center of things and are careless.

Your presence in the center of a pod, whether wading, in a float tube, or in a boat, can also put the pod down. You're making

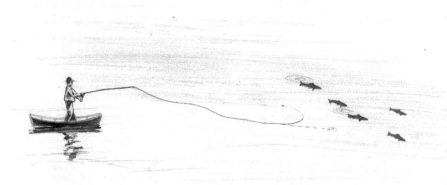

When working a pod of fish, no matter what your form of transportation, try to stay away from the pod, and fish in toward its edges.

waves, and your rod and line are waving in the air overhead. At best, it will move the pod away from you, and you'll wind up having to chase it. That might seem fine, but it means you'll eventually have to fish with longer casts, which are more difficult to control. It will also mean that you're fishing over wary fish, which are harder to fool.

Another advantage to an approach at the edge of a pod is the matter of playing hooked fish. You have a better chance to work one off to the side, or to draw it toward you. Then you can put the pressure on and create the action where it doesn't disturb the remainder of the pod. This is very important. It might mean the difference between catching just one fish and hooking half a dozen or more.

The presentation itself, then, should be to a rise at the periphery of the pod. If the pod is tightly knit, make each cast last awhile. If the same fish that rose does not come right back up and take the fly, another will be along soon. Chances are that more than one trout has marked the fly's arrival. Even at the edge of a pod, however, your line and fly might spook those fish, not attract them. Or it might spook just one fish that happens under the line when it lands, and that trout's reaction might startle others momentarily. It can keep them from taking instantly, which is why you want to let the fly sit until another fish, unspooked, moves into the area.

If the pod continues to work in the area, and you continue to have confidence in your fly, let it sit. That's better than picking it up and rapping it into every new rise-ring. But it's difficult to let it sit for more than a minute or two. At least my attention begins to wander, and I start to fidget. Every succeeding rise is another temptation, and it's good to give in when you feel the fly has been in one place long enough.

But before you pick it up, give it a twitch, then let it be still again. This might get the attention of a trout that has the fly within the window of its vision but hasn't made a move toward it yet. Tempt the fish this way with a twitch or two, then gently pick the fly off the water and make the next cast to the most recent rise.

Of course, if you fish over traveling sedges, you want to retrieve the fly, not let it sit. Do this with a steady lifting of the rod while drawing in line. When the rod is high enough that you feel you'd probably miss a strike if you got one, let the fly rest while you lower the rod and gather in enough line to start again.

If all you get is an absence of action, move up close to the pod and make sure your fly is being seen by some fish. This happens less often than you might think. If your fly is out there and trout are working in the area, it's likely that a lot of them are seeing it, but ignoring it. However, it's best to be sure. My rule is not to change a fly until I'm sure some fish have seen it and refused it.

Sometimes you'll see the refusals. If the water suddenly boils up around your fly, a fish has moved toward it, changed its mind, and turned away. If even a slight disturbance takes place where your fly sits, it's an indication a fish has looked it over and rejected it. These are signs for change.

The first thing to examine is the terminal end of your tackle. Is the leader long enough and fine enough? I'm often guilty of running through a litany of fly changes so that the tippet gets bobbed back to a foot or so. It should be at least 2 feet; a 3- to 4-foot tippet works better on still days, when the surface looks like a mirror. Is the tippet supple enough? It doesn't hurt to break the rules about fly size matched to tippet size. Try going to 5X even if you're using a large fly. Don't hesitate to use 6X, given the strength of modern leader materials.

When you've assured yourself that your gear is right, but the fly is still refused, then it's time to make a change there.

If you haven't collected a specimen of the hatch, try to do it when you start getting refusals Your assumptions might be wrong, as mine were the day I had to go down to a #16 fly with a paler body, even though it cost me fish because my hooks were weak.

Your assumptions about the hatch might be wrong. Look for other insects, perhaps smaller, mixed in with the hatch that you are matching. This happens far more often on streams than on lakes, but the possibility of a masking hatch exists on stillwaters. You need to notice it when it happens. It's more likely you'll discover that the trout are taking a different stage of the same insect: perhaps the emerger rather than the dun, or the nymph rather than the adult.

Look at rise forms. Are they truly surface rises, or do the trout feed so close to the surface that they send a boil to the top without taking there? Many times, when you can't bring trout to a dry, the solution is not a different dry fly but a switch to a subsurface dressing.

Fishing Scattered Rises

Scattered rises usually occur when a hatch takes place over a certain type of bottom, or weed bed, and fish move to that sort of habitat but don't gather into pods. As an example of what I mean, there's a certain lake I fish that has a twenty-foot-wide strip of pondweed growing along one shore for about two hundred yards. At times trout move onto this and feed up and down it in pods. But more often they work the weeds consistently but well spread apart. When they do this, they are usually cruising.

This can happen over any type of bottom, depending on what is hatching or falling to the water. It can even happen out in the open water of the pelagial zone during a windblown terrestrial fall or a hatch of midges.

When it does, you have to treat the trout as individuals rather than as members of a pod. There's quite a bit of difference.

When you fish for an individual trout, you have to get your fly to where the trout is going, not to where it's been. The problem,

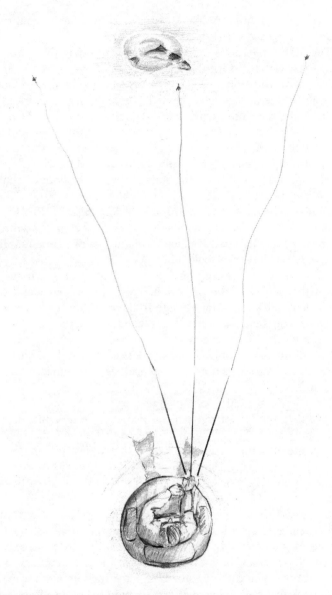

When casting to a single riseform, hit the leading edge of it first, then cast to the right and left of it in an attempt to intercept the trout's movement.

then, is how to figure out where to put your fly when a trout rises within casting range.

The first thing I do is cast to the rings, but not to the center of them. I try, rather, to hit the leading edge of the waves as they spread away from the rise. The first reason is based on what I know about the senses of trout. If I plunk the fly right into the middle of the rise and the fish has not gone far, I'm more likely to frighten it than entice it to the fly. Hit the edge of the rings, and the fly is much more likely to land at the periphery of the trout's vision, attract it over for a look and, with luck, a take.

The second reason to hit the edge of the rise and not its center is based on the knowledge that the trout is moving. But I don't often know which direction it is going, or how fast. Casting to the leading edge of the rise is the most likely way to catch its attention if it's not moving fast, or if it's moving slightly in my direction. If it is not, at least I haven't spooked it.

If it rises again, not only can I cover the new rise, but now I've patterned the fish. I'll know which direction it's going, and can place the fly ahead of it far enough to have the fly there when it arrives. Of course, trout don't always take their exercise in straight lines. But it's the best you can do.

Lots of times a trout fails to take the first cast, at the edge of its rise-rings, and also does not come up again in the immediate area. What then?

First, let it sit a bit—perhaps half a minute. Second, lift it up and cast it to the left or right of the rise about ten or fifteen feet and let it sit again. Third, lift it and place it the same distance in the opposite direction. The hope here is that you can intercept the trout as it travels in one direction or the other. It works more often than doing nothing works. But in truth it fails more often than it works.

Of course, if you can determine the direction of the trout's travels before that first cast, then you have a great advantage. Sometimes you can tell by the rise. If it's close, and you can see the fish, you'll see which way it is moving when it comes up and goes down. At times you can see some hint of a direction in the way the trout's back or tail is going as it takes a natural. More often some intuition might tell you to cast right or left, to your side of the rise or on the far side. If you have these intuitions, follow them.

Most often the rise will catch the corner of your eye, and you won't have any idea which way the trout is going.

If a trout strings out two or three rises in a row, then you should be able to figure out its course without any lessons in geometry. Gauge its direction and speed and place the fly where you expect the next rise to be. Hold on. That is the single rising trout you are most likely to catch.

On one of my best lakes, which I like to fish in fall, the fish have been thinned out to a few large ones – large in this case being 15 or 16 inches, but fat and a lot bigger than they were in spring. They tend to rise in extremely scattered locations, sometimes two or three hundred yards apart.

I'm always tempted to up anchor and chase after the first rise, especially if things are slow where I am, which they usually are on this lake in fall. But I don't. I wait until the fish has risen two or three times before I roar after it. When a fish rises this way, it is usually cruising within an area, at times a large area. I keep an eye out for other rises while I row over. If none happen, I try to stay out at the edge, away from the exact area but close enough so I can cover at least some of it with a long cast. I keep the fly sitting on the water, near where the fish was moving, while I watch for further rises.

If the fish doesn't come up again after a while, then I move in and put a fly exactly where it rose last.

I wouldn't want to be pinned down to a calculation of exactly how often this method is successful. It's not very often. But it is more fruitful than staying in one place on a lake that has a scattered population of willing fish.

One last hint that is dry-fly heresy. If you reach the point of frustration, which I do very often, try retrieving the dry fly through rising trout *as a wet*. It should never work. But sometimes it does. The trout you catch with this dry-fly method will pull a lot harder than the ones you don't catch fishing the dry the way you should fish it.

Don't tell anybody I told you to fish dry flies wet.

9

Nymph Strategies

The forest-rimmed mountain lake stood on a bench beneath a snowy ridge. An early-summer wind gathered cold off the snow, accelerated down the ridge with it, and whipped the lake into unpleasantness. It was almost dark before the day calmed down, so I slipped out for a couple hours of evening fishing.

No trout rose to break the surface. Earlier samplings along the shoreline had revealed great numbers of tiny scuds, too small to imitate. A few olive damselfly nymphs showed up in the same samples, possibly preying on the scuds. They approached large size and a handsome maturity.

The east shore of the twenty-five-acre lake shelved up from water that was eight feet deep with a scattering of pondweed on the bottom to a shallow littoral zone that was sandy and had no rooted vegetation. I rowed the punt into water four feet deep. Then I anchored where I could cast beyond the shelf into the deeper water, out to where the weeds were.

I spooled a wet-tip line, and tied a generic #10 olive nymph to the end of a 6-foot leader. It was modified from a Woolly Bugger, with just a couple of turns of light-brown hackle over the front half of the body, the hackle clipped top and bottom. This fly often fishes well for me when damsels show up in the sampling net.

For the first few casts I let the weighted fly sink a little, then retrieved it with a series of twitches alternated with brief periods in which I allowed it to simply sit and sink again. It's a method that often fools fish when damselflies make their shoreward migration. They swim, then rest, swim again, then rest again. But it didn't work this time, and light was fading fast.

My natural tendency in a case like that is to panic slightly, start changing flies, hoist the anchor and rush off elsewhere, or speed the retrieve so I can cover more water and find the fish faster. But I held fire for some reason and let the fly sink for a count of thirty seconds. Then I brought it creeping back with a hand-twist retrieve. Nothing happened. I increased the count to forty, looking up toward the last light on the snow ridge while the slowly sinking fly ate up lots of what remained of my evening.

I crept the fly back toward the boat again. After a few feet the line took a little dart where it entered the water. I raised the rod and felt the quivering of a trout at the other end. It was small. All of the trout in the lake were small. But they contained an interesting lesson for me that evening.

Fifteen or so of them came flapping into my hand before it became too dark to continue fishing legally. I kept a couple of the largest for breakfast. When it was time to reel up, I got out a flashlight and pocketknife, opened the trout, cleaned them, and laid them in a pan, setting their stomachs aside. Then I got a small pickle-jar lid out of my vest, dipped it over the side to fill it with water, and sliced the tightly packed stomachs into it. I didn't even have to stir it.

The trout were stuffed with a unique cased caddis larva called Leptoceridae. Some of them were still alive, swimming feebly in the light of the flash.

Leptocerids are the only larval caddis that actually swim. Their cases are built of vegetation and have neutral buoyancy. The insect pokes its legs out the front of its case and draws itself along with a six-legged version of the breaststroke. Its legs are tiny compared to the size of its sticklike case; the result of all its efforts is a forward motion that is slight but sufficient to let the larva move about from plant to plant above the bottom.

Apparently that was what was going on, although I had no

**Leptocerids are rare among caddis larvae, in that they swim in open
water rather than crawl among vegetation.**

more evidence than those crammed trout stomachs to prove it.
The caddis might have been making a patient migration toward
shore for pupation and later emergence. Whatever their motivation, they were available to trout down deep, moving slowly. Because their cases were made from the same vegetation on which
they lived, they were a drab olive, just like the generic dressing
I'd chosen because of its resemblance to a damselfly nymph. The
damselfly nymph has its green coloration for a similar reason: It is
camouflage on the plants where it lives.

I'm not constructing a careful case for the imitation of Lepto-
cerid larvae. Far from it. You'll rarely collect them, and even more
rarely find reason to imitate them. But a lot of gadgets creep along
the bottom toward shore for emergence. And a lot more move
from place to place among the pastures of the bottom vegetation.
The average of all this movement is about a #10 to #14 and is the
color of the predominant plant life in the lake.

You can see that it was not an accident when I took a bunch of trout fishing a #10 to #14 generic olive nymph dressing down deep, very slowly.

Fishing successfully on a lake or pond is almost always tied to the activity of some sort of food form. Lots of times the particular form is discovered in retrospect, as I did that evening on the forested lake. This chapter is about exploring stillwaters with nymphs. The goal is to learn what prompts your successes less and less in retrospect and more and more based in advance on what you know about what goes on down where fish do most of their feeding.

WHEN TO FISH THE STILLWATER NYMPH

In a previous chapter I mentioned a case in which the dry fly out-fished a nymph in a situation where trout were not rising. That's an unusual event. In normal times, when trout do not feed visibly, a sunk fly – nymph, wet, or streamer – is the obvious choice.

Because of their resemblance to an abundance of food forms nymphs are the solution more than half the time when you want to fish beneath the surface of a lake or pond. Essentially, you should consider nymphs whenever trout are not rising, and some-times even when they are.

Spring is the time of year when you can rely to the greatest degree on surface activity, and the most likely time to fish dries successfully. But nymphs should be considered during the pre-hatch period, before the daily hatch begins. The hatch period itself is often brief, especially on bright days, which for some reason can compact hatches into an hour or two, leaving the rest of the day barren of rising trout. Switch to nymphs after a hatch is over and you will still find trout restless, cruising and looking for something to eat, and quite willing to take a nymph.

It is no secret, when you fish prehatch activity, that your nymph should be related to whatever insect you expect to hatch. If you await *Callibaetis* mayflies, then try an appropriate nymph dressing to imitate the naturals as they get nervous prior to their eventful trip to the surface. If the lake currently enjoys a damselfly migration, then choose a damsel imitation. The same is true after a hatch: Use a nymph dressing that might jog the trout's memory about what it was eating when the hatch started.

As hatches taper off in the heat of summer, and trout drift down toward the relative coolness of the bottom or the thermocline, nymphs fished deep are about the only way to go. Use the fast or ultrafast sinking line in whatever system you've chosen to explore the levels of a lake. Get the fly down until you've made connection with weeds, the bottom, or a fish.

During midsummer choose flies that are smaller than you think would work best to scout for trout in depth and darkness. After most of the spring hatches have happened, the insects left tend to be smaller. I recently cleaned a fat rainbow caught in late August. It contained several second-generation mayfly nymphs, a few black-midge pupae, and an abundance of planktonic phantom-midge larvae. A single specimen in the trout's diet was larger than a #16. It was an alderfly larva, probably scooting carelessly across the bottom, in a hurry to catch up with confreres that had mostly hatched in June.

In fall, after the turnover, hatches are spotty and often brief. Nymphs are effective whenever trout are not actively feeding on surface fare. Fall is, at least for me, a time when it can take infinite patience to find fish. I always expect to cover lots of water. In truth, it's an excellent time to explore with streamers as well as nymphs. Trout are hungry.

In winter the slow, deep nymph should be your primary exploring tool. Trout are not in the shallows, they are not moving much, and they want a chance to ponder whatever they're about to ingest.

When trout are rising—at any time of year—watch for those times when it seems they are taking adults on the surface but in truth are taking many more nymphs either on the way up or while they hang in the surface film. This often happens during mayfly hatches. Trout usually take from five to ten or more nymphs for every adult. It also happens during midge emergences, when trout disturb the surface while plucking pupae hanging from the rafters.

WHERE TO FISH NYMPHS

There's only one place to *not* fish nymphs and that's below the thermocline when there's no oxygen, and therefore no trout. Nymphs are more effective in some parts of a lake than they are in others. For the most part, locating those places is based on your knowledge about where you would expect to find concentrations of trout in certain conditions.

For example, trout concentrate to feed during the prehatch period of a major insect emergence. You must merely locate the kind of habitat the insect prefers: over a weed bed, along rush edges, or above a shoal, depending on the species. Often it pays to continue with the nymph right into the hatch, or even through it. Most trout rise up to feed on the surface, but the largest of them might stay on the nymphs down deeper.

In spring trout are obviously more often concentrated in shallows, following the feed. In summer they tend toward the depths because insect hatches taper off and temperatures rise to uncomfortable levels in the shallows. If the lake is so high in elevation, or so far north, that it doesn't heat up, then trout will remain in shallow water right through summer. In fall, after the turnover, trout again respond to the movements of food. You might find them in the shallows or back in the depths, depending on what they find to feed on. But the most likely areas are in association with vegetation: either weed beds or sparse plantations of pondweed trailing up from the bottom.

In winter the trout go deep again, and that's where you want to fish your nymphs.

Weed beds are always worth exploring whenever trout can be expected to be active and feeding. But don't spend a lot of time exploring shallow weed beds when fish are deep in midsummer or midwinter. And it's safe to ignore deep weed beds when trout are in the shallows after the spring and fall turnovers.

Springheads are excellent any time temperatures move in either direction toward discomfort levels. Trout move to them in summer for the relative coolness and in winter for the relative warmth. Springs are easy to find in some lakes: They arise so vigorously that vegetation is held back in a circle around them. In most lakes it is difficult to locate a spring. You have to systematically lower a thermometer to the bottom and examine the bottom temperatures over a wide expanse of lake. It takes time, which most of us are reluctant to subtract from time spent exploring with a fly. It's wise to try it occasionally. If you do find a spring, you've almost automatically found trout at one time of the season or another.

Drop-offs along shorelines or at the edges of midwater shoals are excellent places to fish nymphs simply because they attract trout. The nearness of depth and darkness to shallows and potential feeding areas lets trout move from one to another in a more restricted space. That means you can explore for them in a restricted area. In general, fish the deeper side during midday and the shallower side whenever you suspect trout might be up and actively feeding. An excellent plan is to anchor on the shallow side of a ledge, make most of your casts out over the depths beyond it, but drop a cast behind you on occasion. It's surprising how often a trout is intercepted while cruising the shallows when you expect it to be in deep water.

The bottom is always a potential spot to find concentrations of trout in lakes that are oligotrophic and not more than fifteen or twenty feet deep. They are too shallow to stratify. Eutrophic lakes in the same depths tend to have an oxygen-depleted zone of ooze near the bottom, and you want to fish a few feet above it. Explore the bottom more in summer and winter, less in spring and fall.

The thermocline concentrates trout at a specific level during summer stratification. The level might vary from fifteen to forty feet, and the fish will often be scattered throughout the lake at a certain depth. It's often easiest to search by trolling, varying the line type and trolling speed to change the depth of the fly or flies. It's often best to do such exploring with a couple of flies on the leader. It gives the trout a choice.

If trout gather around inlets or outlets, then deliver a nymph to them awash on the current. This can be especially effective if a dry fly fails to bring them up.

STILLWATER NYMPH SELECTION

Fly selection, whenever possible, should be based on something you know the trout have been eating or something you suspect they might have been eating. If you have no direct evidence about what they've been taking, then knowing the predominant foods in the lake is the next best thing.

Knowledge about food forms can take a somewhat esoteric and Latinly turn; you might be aware that the dominant mayfly in one lake is a *Callibaetis*, in another a *Siphlonurus*. Or the knowledge might be grounded more in what you can hold in your hand and see. If you know that one lake contains mostly olive scuds

When trout aren't active – or even if they are – do some snooping in the surface film. What you learn will help you catch trout later.

while another grows largely gray ones, you've helped yourself just as much as you will by memorizing the wing venation of sixty separate species of gnats. Perhaps more.

In stillwater fly-fishing the broader view is often just as important as the view of a narrow slice of things. You want to be able to step onto the shore of a lake and look at it sweepingly, and to be able to tell something about the kinds of insects it would hold. But you also want to snoop around and collect where you can. That doesn't mean you should try to take a thorough sample from each depth in each lake you encounter. But it does mean you should attempt to do some observing and collecting when you arrive at a new lake or pond, when the trout foods it holds might still be a mystery to you.

If you have a collecting net, sweep it through shoreline vegetation. If you don't have one, grab a handful of the same weeds and lift them out of the water. If the weeds are widely spaced, reach down and shake a stem, or boot one with your toe, and see what swims away with an impatient look over its shoulder.

You can't collect in all the water of a lake, although there are methods for sampling the bottom even in the deepest profundal zones. Short of that, it's important to have an understanding of the major food forms in lakes and the types of habitat they prefer. In the chapters on the foods in Part 3 pay particular attention to the preferred homes of the foods. That knowledge will help you read a lake, and to select a fly to fish the lake.

I've mentioned a box of favorite flies. In nymph fishing it's extremely critical to have some favorites, since you usually have to start fishing with only a few clues beyond what you can observe of the water and of the insect life around the rim of its shoreline. You have to pin some hopes on something; you have to have faith in the fly you select. A box of favorites, most of them based on one food form or another, all of them with histories of having caught fish for you, will let you explore stillwaters with flies in which you have a remarkable degree of confidence.

A brief list of my own favorite nymphs for exploring lakes would include imitations of the major foods. I use a #10 or #12 Carey Special partly because it looks like a dragonfly nymph. Over a long period of years trout have shown a tendency to whack it whenever I tow it around slowly behind my boat or float tube. I use a #12 or #14 Gray Nymph in part because it imitates gray scuds and a few other things, but in larger part because it has caught a lot of stillwater trout for me.

The TDC, #12 through #16, finds perhaps the favored spot in my box of favorites. Its full name – Thompson's Delectable Chironomid – tells most of its story. It is black, and a high percentage of the midge pupae I've collected from lakes have been black. I use it often by itself. But if I am ever caught searching the water with two flies, which is often, the TDC will be found on the dropper no matter which fly is found on the point.

I use the Zug Bug and Gold-Ribbed Hare's Ear in #12 through #16, although these find application more often on moving water than still. However, they resemble a lot of different food forms and, between the two of them, take a lot of fish for me. I wouldn't want to be without them when approaching a lake I'd never fished before.

Damselflies are found on almost every stillwater, and they're almost always some shade of green. The fly I carry to fish for them has no name, at least not that I know about. It's the modified Olive

Some favorite lake nymphs: (top, left to right) Carey Special, Gray Nymph, TDC, Zug Bug; (bottom) Gold Ribbed Hare's Ear, Modified Woolly Bugger, Olive Woolly Bugger, Olive Scud.

Woolly Bugger that I've already mentioned, tied on long-shank #10 and #12 hooks. The tail is marabou, the body is chenille, and the hackle is brown hen wrapped sparsely over the front third of the fly and clipped top and bottom. Leave the hackle fully palmered and unclipped and you have a regulation Woolly Bugger, which is one fly I'd never be without.

I tie the Olive Woolly with about fifteen turns of fine lead wire wrapped around its fuselage. This is not heavily weighted if you use lead that's not quite the diameter of the hook shank. It gets the fly under the surface on a fast retrieve with a floating line, which is just what I want it to do. If it's fished with a sinking line, then it gets the fly down at least even with the line, perhaps slightly below it. But it is not so much lead that it kills the action of the fly.

The Olive Woolly Bugger should likely be listed as a streamer, which I'll do later because most often I fish it as a streamer. But I fish it just as often now with its tails pinched back to half an inch or so, which in my view makes it a nymph. At least I fish it as a nymph whenever I find dragonflies in the water.

An Olive Scud in #10 through #14 rounds out this abbreviated list, which is far from my full list of stillwater nymphs. It is weighted, like many of my lake nymphs, with eight to ten turns of lead wire that is slightly undersized for the hook shank that it's on. This gets the fly down slowly when I want to fish it on a dry line but leaves the option of choosing my depth by choosing the sink rate of the line. If the fly were so heavily weighted that it plunged abruptly, it would fish right in some situations but entirely wrong in others. I prefer to weight flies lightly and keep more options open.

Over the years you will develop a list of your own favorite dressings, and a list of strategies to go with them. They will become your own starting points when you approach a lake or pond. Mine will be revealed slowly throughout this book. Yours should be different, should be based on your own experiences, and should be revealed slowly to you over the years as you fish stillwaters.

NYMPHING TACKLE

Tackle is simple, since you don't want to carry a battery of rods that requires you to hire a caddy. I've mentioned that I like to keep two rods strung if space permits it. When I can't, then I think it's important to carry a single outfit that allows the maximum flexibility. That means a longish rod for a 6- or 7-weight line system, no matter the kind of system you choose to fish all the depths.

Leader length for nymphing should vary with the sink rate of the line fished. The deeper you go, the shorter the leader should be in order to keep your fly in the same plane as the end of the line. For a floating line, when the idea is to sink the fly but not the line, the leader should be 8 to 12 feet long. With a sinking line in a moderate sink rate a leader 6 to 8 feet long is usually about right.

When the line is extra-fast-sinking, then cut the leader back to between 4 and 6 feet long. There's no use getting the line down to the depth you want, then letting a long leader trail the fly five feet above it. But this has to be modified at times. I've had it happen often that adding a 3- to 4-foot tippet, no matter what line I fished, suddenly made trout become interested in my fly. It works often enough that you should be aware of it, and try it when the standard leader for a certain depth fails to fool fish that you are pretty sure are down there and active.

Ideally, the fly should be weighted for some situations, unweighted for others. But I'm too lazy to tie two versions of each fly in each hook size. Even if I did, they'd soon be tangled together in my fly boxes and I wouldn't know which was weighted and which was not. So, as I mentioned earlier, I tie most of my nymphs moderately weighted, and depend on link sink rate and leader length to determine what level the fly will fish.

The key concern with tackle for nymphing is the line system that lets you fish the various depths and a rod that will let you cast the system comfortably all day long.

STILLWATER NYMPHING METHODS

Once you've chosen a fly pattern related to a food form, then the remaining factors to figure out are depth fished and speed of retrieve. A lot of your judgment here is based on where the natural would live and what it would be found doing most of the time.

If *Siphlonurus* mayflies are dominant and about to hatch, and you're going to fish a Near Enough as being near enough to a match for their nymphs, then you want to present it in the shallows alongside reed stems and emergent grasses, and with considerable action. *Siphlonurus* nymphs are vigorous swimmers. They migrate to shore and crawl out of the water before the dun escapes the nymphal shuck.

On the opposite hand, if you've chosen a dressing to match a dragonfly nymph of the silter variety with a Carey Special or an abbreviated Woolly Bugger, you would want it near the bottom or as close to a weed bed as you can get it. You'd want to fish it slowly, since silters camouflage themselves on the bottom and wait for prey to come to them or creep along stalking it.

Methods for the Subsurface Area

Tackle for fishing just subsurface can be light. I normally use the same gear I would use for fishing hatches or nymphs on a spring creek or small freestone stream. For me that is an 8- to 8½-foot rod balanced to a 4- or 5-weight line. Because I often want to cover some distance while nymphing, I usually arm the rod with a weight-forward floating line.

The leader should be no shorter than about 8 feet long; 10 feet is better. I usually start with a standard 10-foot leader in 4X, then add a finer tippet section to it if the fly is smaller than a #14, making the leader even longer. If all of your gear is in balance, casting such a long leader will not be a problem. If your rod, or your casting stroke, will not allow you to turn over the longer leader, you're far better off casting a leader you can handle than you are casting a long and fine leader that piles up at the end of the cast.

When your goal is to dangle a fly, such as a midge pupa, either in the film or just under it, then grease your leader with line dressing or fly floatant down to the last eight to twelve inches. Be sure to stretch all the kinks out of your leader; it's critical when you fish with a slow retrieve, although your fly will be so close to the surface that you can often see the boil of a take, and set the hook as you would with a dry. When the take is not visible, you'll have to watch your line tip. Coils in a leader can delay the message of a take by two or three feet. As you will discover, that is far too late when fishing stillwaters because there is never a current to draw the hook into the fish and hold it there while you get around to setting the hook.

It's often best to grease all but the last few inches of your leader, and fish a nymph, such as a midge pupa pattern, just under the film.

The first method for fishing near the top with a nymph is no method at all. Just cast the fly out and let it sit like a dry fly. Watch the line tip for the jump that signals a take. You will not always feel it, although it is surprising, when fishing the nymph with no retrieve at all, how often you feel a sudden sullen tug against your rod tip.

This method is much more effective than it's given credit for being. The reason is simple: It's not often used. It is difficult to be patient and just let your fly sit out there and do nothing. I find it hard enough with a dry fly, which I can at least watch. With a subsurface nymph there's nothing to watch but the line tip, which isn't very exciting—until it takes a sudden dart. Patience, when fishing this way, will pay off.

Rick Hafele and I once fished a small mountain lake briefly with Dr. Burt Covert of La Grande, Oregon. We were on noon break from a two-day workshop that Rick and I were giving at the college there. Burt drove us quickly up to a lake nestled in the hills above town. While Rick and I collected insects in the shallows to take back and show our students, Burt rigged a dry line, long leader, and a midge nymph. He cast it out onto the wind-chopped surface and retrieved it without result.

On the next cast Burt let the fly sit a moment. He had a hit before he could begin his retrieve. He missed the strike and had no others while he hand-twisted the fly slowly back to shore. On the following cast he had a strike again before he began his retrieve. A little spout of water shot up into the wind, and the line tip shot forward a foot. The take was visible even among the waves.

Before long Burt was simply casting the fly out and letting it sit, with no intention to retrieve it at all. On every cast a spurt of water would fly up, and he would cause a trout to come up and dance over the wind-riffled water.

When you consider the behavior of a midge pupa, it is easy to see why this method would work. The natural drifts slowly from the bottom to the top. Then it simply dangles there. If the surface is still, the midge suspends itself from the film until it is able to break through. If the surface is rough, as it was that day, then they break through it almost instantly because a broken surface has little surface tension. Most of them are taken by trout in those last few inches, just before they enter the waves on their way to the aerial world.

A second method is the hand-twist retrieve, and this is probably the one most used when fishing subsurface. Again, the reason is simple: It keeps the fly out there a long time on each cast and moves it along slowly in the manner of many naturals. But it also gives you the feeling that you're coaxing the fish, and it keeps you in contact with your fly. A word of caution here: Don't use the hand-twist when the fly should be fished at rest with no retrieve at all. I've done it a thousand times, giving the fly some movement that I think is attractive to trout, when in truth what it's doing is putting them off from a fly that should be fished on the sit.

The hand-twist retrieve is most effective when used with flies that represent insects that swim feebly – again, mostly the midges. Almost all other stillwater forms have some fairly strong powers of locomotion when they near the surface film. Caddis pupae that hatch out in the open propel themselves to the top quickly. So do mayfly nymphs. Dragonfly nymphs don't often get near the top. Damselfly nymphs do, and their swimming motion is a combination of laborious swimming with short bursts of speed and stops to rest. The hand-twist is effective for them, although it should be combined with occasional strips and long pauses. If you're fishing damsel nymphs with this method, the intermediate line might be better than a floater, to accommodate the faster parts of the retrieve.

The hand-twist is executed by alternately wrapping the line around your little finger, then your index finger, rolling it over and over, pulling in about four to five inches of line each time. Various rates of retrieve work, but, in general, the slower you can get yourself to do it, the more it will interest the trout. One reason the slow hand-twist works well is that it keeps the fly out there in the water longer on each cast, maximizing the chance a trout will come across it and take it.

You can cause the fly to creep along at a steady pace with the hand-twist by rolling the line with a fluid motion of your line hand. You can also cause it to hop along in little darts by popping the little finger down abruptly on each twist of the hand. The roll from the index finger gathers slack, the quick downward movement of the little finger causes the fly to swim ahead a few inches, then stop. This can be extremely effective when fishing patterns such as back swimmers and water boatmen. It also can be combined with a rhythmic twitching of the rod tip, which increases the staccato swimming of the nymph.

A slow strip is the next method, and it can copy either the patient steady swimming of the hand-twist, or a jerky dart-and-stop movement that is common among insects migrating just under the surface toward an emergence on shore. This method is effective for all sorts of insects: caddis pupae, mayfly and damselfly nymphs, back swimmers, and water boatmen. It gives the fly a motion that trout are used to seeing in lots of the food forms they make a living eating. The slow strip can remind trout of something they've seen recently, and the movement can prompt a strike even when the fly is all wrong. That is likely why attractor patterns, when fished right, take fish even though they look like nothing in nature.

Again, you can add twitching of the rod tip to the slow strip retrieve and increase the jerky swimming of the fly. To do this, make slow strips with the line hand while pulsing the rod with your rod hand. This is perhaps the most effective method for fishing water-boatman dressings along undercut banks.

The fast strip is getting out of the province of nymph fishing near the surface, but there are times to do it. During damselfly migrations try combining the fast strip with periods in which you let the fly pause. Back swimmers propel themselves along boldly, especially when they reach maturity at around one-half inch long and lose their fear of most predators. A Prince Nymph retrieved with long strips, then allowed to sit, swims a lot like them.

But the fast strip is most effective when applied at the next level down – the middepths.

Methods for Middepths

The first consideration, when fishing with your fly at depths between two to about five feet, is how to get it there. The full range of options to get the fly down begins with the floating or intermediate line, a long leader, and a weighted fly. But this option is only open with a slow retrieve. If you use a surface line and retrieve fast, the fly will ride up out of the middepths.

The wet-tip line is the second option and allows a slow to moderately fast retrieve. It gets the fly down while most of the line floats, which has real value as we'll see in a moment.

A full-sinking line with a slow sink rate will also get the fly down to middepths. You can use the same kind of line in a fast-sink rate and begin your retrieve when the fly has reached the depth you want. This allows you to use a fast retrieve without causing the fly to ride up. But you have to keep the fly moving or it will sink beneath the level you want.

The final option is the shooting head. If you use a system of shooting lines, then the slow-sinking head will get you to middepths and fish the fly just right.

Although I carry a system of lines that includes a floater and sinker among its shooting heads, I much prefer to fish a wet-tip line if it will get the fly down to where I want it. The floating part of the line is easier to handle on a cast, and it tangles less often than thinner running line behind a shooting head. The wet-tip line also keeps you in much closer touch with the fly on the retrieve. With a shooting-head system, or with full-sinking lines, your only contact with the fly is what you can feel. With a wet tip you'll often see a take when the running line takes a jump where it enters the water.

Once you get the fly to the depth you want, the types of retrieves need no repetition. They are the same used when you fish subsurface, from letting the fly sit to the hand-twist retrieve, the slow strip, strip and twitch, and the fast strip. Again, the retrieve used should be related to the fly chosen.

You can add another retrieve if you use a floating line and weighted fly. Cast out and let the fly sink to the level you want. Then lift the rod and swim the fly up toward the line tip and the surface. This imitates the behavior of rising midge and caddis pupae, and some mayfly nymphs. It can be very effective in the middepths during preemergence periods.

Methods for the Depths

Again, the first consideration is how to get the fly down to the depths you want. The options narrow as you go deeper. A floating line, or even a wet tip, won't do it except in a narrow range of conditions.

The first and narrowest option is a floating line, weighted fly, and extremely long leader: 20 to 25 feet. This will get you down into the ten- to fifteen-foot range if you fish the fly with no retrieve at all, merely letting it slowly sink and then rest when it finds its depth. This method has its applications in midge fishing and is best used with a boat or tube that drifts gently on an almost windless lake. If you are moving at all, the movement will cause the fly to ride up.

The next option is the wet-belly or wet-head line in your array of sinkers, if the system you choose includes floating/sinking lines with the full range of sinking characteristics. The line you use

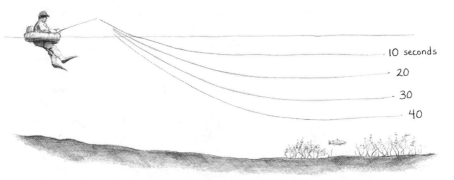

10 seconds

20

30

40

By varying the count as your nymph sinks, you can greatly change the depth at which it is presented to the trout.

should be either fast sinking or super-fast, depending on the depth you want.

If your system for exploring depths is built around full-sinking lines, then you will want to use the fast-sinking line to get you down in the eight- to twelve-foot range. Use the super-fast-sinking line for anything beyond that depth.

When using shooting heads, the systems are roughly the same as they are with full-sinking lines. Use the fast-sinking head to get down toward the bottom in lakes ten to fifteen feet deep, and the extra-fast line to explore below that.

Depth fished, of course, is always related to sink time. If you begin your retrieve immediately with a cannonball line, it will not achieve much depth.

Use the countdown method to get the line to the depth you want. Count fifteen seconds at first, beginning your retrieve at a speed that suits the fly you've chosen. Watch for signs of weeds on the hook, or slight pulls that mean you're touching bottom. The ultimate signal of the right depth, of course, is a tug from a trout. If you don't receive any of the signals, increase the count in increments of five seconds until you're fishing as far down as the depth of the lake and your own patience allow. If you find weeds, or the bottom, then shorten the count a few seconds and begin covering some water.

Some brief notes apply to fishing down deep. The longer you can cast, the more line you can get down to the depth you want, and the longer you can keep your fly in the zone that holds trout. That is one reason I like a shooting-head system for the deepest water: I can shoot lots of line, let the head sink, then make a retrieve that has the fly in the depth I want for the maximum number of moments.

If you use a floating line and long leader to achieve depth, or even a combination floating/sinking line with a long-sinking head, you can't keep your fly in the deep zone if you use a fast retrieve. A full-sinking line is best for the fast retrieve because it keeps the entire line level at the same depth. The fly does not climb toward the surface on a fast retrieve until it gets near the boat or your tube.

If your boat or tube is flinging along with the wind, your whole system gets pulled up by the speed of the movement. Wind-drifting is an excellent way to explore water, but make sure your line sink rate is increased to keep the fly down where you want it.

If you fish the depths and get a take, you've either encountered a cruiser or hit a school. Always assume you've located some fish. Use the same fly, the same retrieve, at the same depth to explore the immediate area thoroughly. Drop an anchor if you're boating, or hold yourself in the same location with your fins if you're tubing. If nothing more happens, move about a hundred feet but try to remain in the same area at least long enough to feel that you've given the trout a chance.

One of the most difficult, and frustrating, tasks in fly-fishing lakes is keeping in touch with a school of trout that is moving in the depths. Perhaps it validates the use of electronics; a bass boat is perfect when fishing nymphs on big, deep water.

10

Wet Fly Strategies

Wet flies take second rank to nymphs and streamers when it comes to fishing stillwaters with something sunk. The other forms are more often tied to imitate natural trout foods, and are therefore more often considered when it comes to selecting a fly. But wets do a better job imitating a few types of insects. And there are times when they work better as exploratory dressings than either nymphs or streamers.

Wet flies are the best imitations for adult alderflies. These are blocky characters and they sink when they land on the water. But they still have all of their wings and other appendages attached, so that a clean-lined nymph doesn't look at all like them. A streamer doesn't move at all like them. But a wet Alder, when fished slowly, is the perfect imitation.

The Carey Special, a brushy wet tied with hackle wound from a pheasant's rump, is the standard dragonfly nymph imitation. It does an excellent job, and in its smaller sizes has become a first fly for me in certain situations. For example, I love to tow one slowly around a lake whenever trolling seems the best way to search for the scene of some action. Soft-hackled wets, without wings, do an excellent job representing various caddis pupae.

I use a Hare's Ear Wet to imitate *Callibaetis* nymphs in the period before, and sometimes even during, major hatches of this widespread mayfly. If the natural nymphs are brown, I use the Hare's Ear in its standard tan color. If they are olive, which they often are, then I use a Hare's Ear tied olive. This fly shouldn't work, because the naturals don't have their wings unfurling when they swim to the surface for emergence. But I've found that the Hare's Ear Wet takes more fish for me than a precisely imitative nymph dressing, so what can I do but stick with it?

Wets do not always have to imitate specific insects in order to take trout, however. They are more useful as representations of something good to eat swimming by in the path of a hungry trout. They are excellent simply for searching the water.

WHEN TO USE WETS

It's best to fish wet flies when the season, time of day, and weather predict that trout should be up high in the water column and actively looking for food, but no visible activity is going on at the lake or pond. They're also effective when a few fish are rising, but trout feed too sporadically and too scattered to enable you to key

A selection of favorite wets: (top, left to right) Black Gnat, Alder, Hare's Ear; (bottom) Blue Dun, McGinty, Carey Special.

in on a specific dry or nymph that will take them. A wet, fished diligently, will cross enough paths to interest some trout.

That means wets work best in spring and early summer, when insects are active, but at specific moments when no hatch is happening. They also work well in fall, after the autumn turnover, whether a hatch is happening or not. At these seasons, and under these conditions, trout cruise expectantly and can be conned into taking something that looks like it might be good to eat.

Wets are not enormously effective when lakes are in thermal stratification and trout are holding in the depths. Nor are they of much use when trout are holding deep in winter, largely dormant. Nymphs fished slowly and deep, or streamers teased through the depths, are more effective at those times of year.

WHERE TO USE WET FLIES

Wets work best wherever the water is shallow enough that a trout holding anywhere in the water column will be able to see and intercept them. Because you'll be fishing wets from a few inches deep down to about three feet deep, that usually means the trout will have to rise to strike them. That's the reason wet flies are most effective in water from three to about five or six feet deep.

Ideal water has some features to it. Wet flies take trout for me when fished around woody debris such as submerged limbs and logs. I've used them to draw trout up from shallow weed beds, along the edges of cattail and reed forests, and in the openings between sprinklings of lily pads. They're great in the shallows along the edges of a lake or pond, when trout are in that kind of water. They work well over any midwater shoals that aren't more than six feet deep. At times they're effective along the edges of trenches and drop-offs, but only when the trout are on the high side or hungry enough to spear upward from the deep side.

Wet flies are usually my first choice on any small lake or pond when the weather is warm enough to activate insects but the trout are not seeing any specific insect enough to be selective. A wet fly in such a situation offers a small enough bite that it won't turn trout away, as streamers sometimes do, but also allows you to use a fairly fast retrieve so you can explore lots of water to find the fish when they aren't showing themselves.

Wet flies work well on small ponds with lots of shallows, where you don't want to fish deep because of all the snags.

A BASIC SELECTION OF WETS

Almost all of the wet flies that I use are based on one natural or another, although they are not always fished in direct response to an overwhelming presence of that exact natural. But flies that look like something I know trout have eaten recently give me more confidence. Over the years I've had positive responses to a narrow selection of wets. They're the ones I reach for simply because they've caught fish in the past, and I expect they'll do it again.

A favorite, because I live in timber country and fish a lot of small lakes surrounded by alder trees, is the wet Alder in #10 and #12. Another is the Black Gnat in #12 and #14. It bears a remarkable resemblance to a flying black ant. I don't know if that's exactly why it catches fish, but it does. The Hare's Ear Wet and the olive version of the same fly, both in #12 through #16, take trout for me whenever *Callibaetis* mayfly nymphs are active, which is most of the long fly-fishing season.

A #12 to #14 Blue Dun entertains quite a few trout each season, especially when mayfly spinners are out and dancing over the water. But it works best at these times on unsophisticated trout.

When stillwater trout get selective to spinners, they can be maddening, and wet flies won't solve it. A McGinty in #8 and #10 represents a bumblebee and works surprisingly well, although I've never been able to decide if it works because trout take lots of the naturals or just because it's an attractive fly that I can fish with confidence.

A #10 or #12 Carey Special, with its olive chenille body and sparse pheasant-rump hackle, looks a bit like a lot of aquatic creatures. It surprises more trout for me than almost any other wet fly. It's a dressing that I reach for most often when I'm trolling, and fishing deep, which is the subject of a different chapter.

TACKLE FOR FISHING WET FLIES

Tackle for wet flies is simply what you've been using to fish dry, with the fly snipped off the end and replaced with a wet. The goal in tackle selection is to fish the fly from a few inches deep down to two or three feet. I normally use a floating line and the same leader I would use to fish a dry fly in the same situation. A wet-tip line is often an improvement, not so much for the depth it allows you to attain as for the fast retrieve you can use without causing the fly to ride up through the surface film. I've seldom drawn a fish to a wet fly that was riding so shallow that it left a wake.

The rod should be your dry-fly rod, ideally 8 to 9 feet long and balanced to a 4- to 6-weight line. When I choose to tie on a wet, it is almost always on the light rod that is armed with a floating or wet-tip line, not the heavy rod armed with the shooting-head system. I'm seldom trying for distance or depth with a cast wet, although I often try for both when trolling a wet.

The leader should be 8 to 10 feet long and tapered to a tippet that will turn over the size fly chosen. For me that is normally a 4X point, at times 5X in clear water. I would go to 3X in cloudy water, when expecting large fish. I would likely switch to something imitative, such as a nymph, before I would refine my leader to 6X.

WET FLY METHODS

The usual use of the wet fly is to search the water in order to locate trout. When using it to probe cover, cast as near to the feature as you can, but don't cast so the line crosses the lie you expect to hold a fish. You'll spook it. Instead, present the fly to the near side of the cover first in an attempt to show the fly to a fish and tempt it into moving out to take it. Failing that, put the fly right over the cover next, but again without lining it.

Probe the cover from every direction you can before you haul off and throw the fly clear past it and retrieve back over it. But be sure to do that as a last resort; often a fly swimming toward the cover rather than away from it is just what the trout ordered.

Vary your speed of retrieve around the cover. Use slow strips, fast strips, and the strip-and-twitch method to show the fly to fish in a variety of ways.

Covering unfeatured water, as opposed to covering a specific lie, requires a different approach. The goal becomes showing the fly across as broad an area as you can. Use yourself as the center of a circle and cast to all of the angles around you. If you're wading, start by casting parallel to one shore and work in an arc out around you until you're casting parallel to the opposite shore. Then move until you can cover a new arc.

When you're in a boat or tube, cast in a full circle around it. If one side is shallow and the other deep, continue on around; you might discover that I am full of beans and the fish are fifteen feet down but still willing to arrow up and take a wet drawn over their heads. It's not likely, but you have to search all of the options. Again, vary your speed of retrieve and change your position as soon as you've covered all the water you can reach from your first station.

It often works to cover rises with a wet fly even when trout feed on the surface. What's going on up top is sometimes just an indication of more going on down below. I'll fish a wet right through a hatch as long as trout continue to show some interest in it and neglect drys.

If you're covering rises with a wet, then let the fly sit for a few seconds after it lands. It's surprising how many trout will take it before you begin a retrieve. Often they insist on taking it on the sink and will not touch it once it moves. Usually you'll be able to detect the take by the boil; the trout takes so near the surface that it's almost as visible as a rise to a dry. At other times fish take a little deeper and so subtly that you have to watch where your leader enters the water for some shift in its angle into the water, or you have to watch the line tip for some slight dart.

When fishing wets to feeding trout, and they refuse the fly on the sit, use a very slow retrieve, at least at first. This accomplishes two things. First, it shows the fly to the fish moving slowly, more in line with the way a natural insect might move. Second, it dangles your fly a lot longer out where the fish are and increases the chances that one will intercept it.

If the slow retrieve fails, then try the same sequence of retrieves described for fishing a nymph: a hand-twist, slow strip, strip-and-twitch, and finally a fast strip.

That's about it. Wet-fly fishing in stillwater is fly-fishing at its most basic. It takes a lot of fish for me, and it can for you, too, without a lot of complications.

Perhaps that's why I consider it so much fun.

11

Streamer Strategies

Streamers were traditionally featherwings and bucktails tied to imitate baitfish and trout fry. But that has expanded; these days streamers are tied just as often with marabou, mohair, or rabbit fur to imitate leeches and the largest insects.

Featherwings, such as the famous old Gray Ghost, typically represent larger baitfish such as smelts or shiners. Bucktails, such as the Black-Nose Dace and Little Brown Trout, are generally used to imitate smaller minnow-type fish and fry of the various trout species.

Marabou is more lively in the water and is used more and more as we make closer study of the food forms fed on by trout. Patterns such as the Black Marabou Muddler and the various colors of the Woolly Bugger swim like crayfish, pollywogs, baby snakes, and those wonderful ugly leeches. As examples, I've taken stomach samples this summer from large trout caught on a sage-lined desert lake, a forested mountain pond, and a Canadian lake so vast it was almost surrounded by the horizon. Each of the stomach samples contained a variety of aquatic insects and crustaceans. But each also contained at least a couple of leeches.

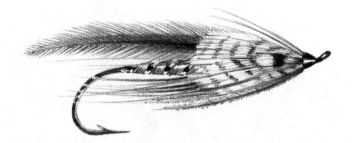

The famous Gray Ghost streamer.

All of those trout intercepted #10 Olive Woolly Buggers.

A streamer might remind a trout of something it has eaten recently. It might also simply suggest something good to eat and greatly enticing sneaking past or fleeing for escape, depending on how you retrieve the fly. Streamers are big bites, and they appeal to the predatory instincts of trout. They incite lots of strikes.

WHEN TO USE STREAMERS

The first situation in which to use streamers is in the obvious presence of some sort of food that they best represent. For example, on the trip to that large Canadian lake it was early September and kokanee were just beginning to gather far outside river mouths for their annual spawning run. The baitfish hadn't moved in yet, but schools of Kamloops rainbows, some well over 20 inches long, were expecting the news at any moment. They had already moved to the river deltas to enjoy cutting them off.

A couple of weeks later we would have been able to cast 5-inch kokanee imitations to goose lots of trout up into the air. As it was, we collected leeches from weed beds near the river entrances and used Woolly Buggers to spur an occasional trout to dance.

Streamers are just as effective in large eastern lakes when smelts make their spring run to spawn in the shallows or inlet streams. It's the best time of the year to take landlocked Atlantic salmon.

Streamers are also effective when trout have moved up into the shallows in response to spring turnover and the new abundance of aquatic insect feed there. Like searching wet flies,

Fishing streamers on long casts over weed beds, or off the entrances of river mouths, is an excellent way to intercept schools of cruising trout.
Jim Schollmeyer

streamers work best early and late in the day, before and after hatch periods. Trout hang out around any cover they can find while waiting for something to happen. If a streamer trots by, they are often glad to dash out and rap it.

I discovered this to my own embarrassment after many years spent fishing a favorite local lake. It was my habit in the spring to hit the *Callibaetis* mayfly hatch whenever I could. I'd be on the lake most of the day but would idle away the hours before the hatch started, casting a nymph or a dry but not catching many trout. Sometimes I'd just read a book and scan the water between pages, looking for rises. The trout, it turned out, were idling away the same time, although I don't believe they were reading books.

A couple of springs ago I returned from a trip to Montana's Bighorn River. Friends and I had been pounding the banks with #8 and #10 Woolly Buggers whenever the anchor was up and we were drifting from one favored spot to another. Lots of trout came to flies fished this way, and they were some of the largest caught on a trip that was otherwise devoted to matching minute hatches.

The next time out on my favorite lake I tried the same tactic while waiting for the mayflies to hatch. I rowed quietly along in my pram, keeping it about sixty feet out from shore. I used a floating line, long leader, and a #10 Olive Woolly Bugger. Each cast was placed tight against the shoreline. The fly was allowed to sit for just a second or two, then roped in on a fast retrieve. Sometimes a trout whacked it before I could begin to move it. Most of the action came around some sort of cover: a fallen log, a tangle of limbs, a bed of rocks on the bottom, or a weed bed. I released sixteen trout before the hatch began, on a lake I thought I knew well.

Streamers can work wonders whenever trout are cruising at random and rising sporadically. The fishing prior to the kokanee gathering in Canada was an example of that. The trout were restless and traveling in loose schools. We'd see an occasional broad-shouldered rise, but casting dries was a waste of time. We cast streamers instead, patiently covering the water in front of us until a fish happened by. That was often enough to keep us casting and happy.

This kind of movement takes place most often in spring, early summer, and fall, when trout are most active. It happens less often in midsummer and in winter, when trout are deeper and have their engines shut down.

Streamers work at least as well as, and often better than, other kinds of flies when trout hold out in the pelagic depths. They have a choice then between feeding on plankton or feeding on the fishes that feed on the plankton. Normally trout are happier to see something in the larger size.

WHERE TO FISH STREAMERS

Streamers are often exploratory flies. You shouldn't place limits on where you'll use them, or you'll find fish only in the locations of your preconceptions. That's not the only place trout are found, and you will enlarge your notions if you let streamers lead you where they will at times.

If you know where trout are hanging out, or have good reasons to suspect you'll find them in a certain type of water in certain conditions, then you should start there, even if you end up someplace else. Try the shallows and the shoreline in spring.

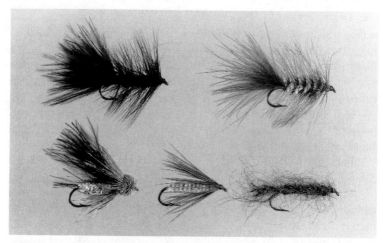

A narrow selection of streamers: (top, left to right) Black Woolly Bugger, Olive Woolly Bugger; (bottom) Black Marabou Muddler, Carey Special, Mohair Leech. *Jim Schollmeyer*

The pelagic depths will produce most often in summer, either along the bottom in relatively shallow lakes or just above the thermocline in deeper lakes. In fall trout often hang out around the edges of drop-offs. At certain times of day, especially at dawn and dusk, they can be found up on the flats, feeding on the shallow side of the abrupt drop. It's best then to scout that side, either visually if you can see into the water or with your fly if you can't.

When the sun is high and trout are exposed to predation from osprey and angler, they're more likely to be over the edge, down in the depths, but still where they can see upward several feet. It's best then to anchor a few feet back into the shallows from the drop and cast as far beyond it as you can. Use a sinking line and give it some time to get the fly down. Then experiment with various retrieves, moving from time to time along the ledge, until you've found the fish and what they want.

TACKLE FOR STREAMERS

Tackle should be stout when you're tossing big flies around. If you've chosen one rod for a light dry line and wet-tip backup, and another rod for the system you use to explore various depths, then this system rod will be best for fishing streamers. This is especially true since you will often want to fish your streamers at different depths.

My system rod, at 8½ feet and balanced to a 7-weight shooting-head system, would be considered at the light end of the spectrum by most folks who fish streamers a lot. But I tend to fish with downsize streamers most of the time, casting #8, #10, and #12 flies in the same situations when others would cast a #4 or a #6. I don't do this so I can catch more fish; instead, I use smaller flies so I can have more fun casting them with light gear.

When I go to the bruisers, big heavily weighted streamers that look like piles of brush but also catch big fish, I'm handicapped by my rod. It could be an 8-weight and serve me better at times. I wouldn't want it any heavier than that or the situations in which I would use it would get too limited, and it would no longer be a versatile outfit.

I don't limit myself to the heavy rod for streamer fishing. At least half the time I prefer to use the wet-tip line on my light rod and cast smaller streamers with that. I use the heavy rod when I want to use a faster sinking line to get the fly down farther.

Lines should be heavy enough to loft whatever streamer you've chosen. It helps if their weight is stacked toward the front because it makes controlling the fly in flight easier. Weight-forward lines and shooting heads do it best. If you fish streams as well as lakes, which I sincerely hope you do, and you prefer light double-taper lines for most of your fishing, then you can fish small to medium streamers without any sort of switch, just a slight compromise in distance.

But you'd be wise to add a weight-forward sink-tip to your equipment. For some reason the wet tip takes more fish with streamers even if you can contrive to fish the fly at the same depth and speed with a floating line.

Leaders should be on the strong side to turn over the larger flies you'll be casting and to help subdue the larger trout you hope to be catching. The leader tippet should balance the fly size cast. I covered this balance in a chart in the earlier chapter on gearing up.

If you're going to violate the recommendations, do it on the high side with a tippet that's too stout rather than too light.

Leader length should be in accordance with the line type used. For a floating line, 8 to 10 feet is about right for streamer fishing. With a wet-tip or slow-sinking line the leader should be 6 to 8 feet long. For the faster sinking lines shorten the leader to between 4 and 6 feet. But there are times, even when fishing deep, that a couple of feet of extra tippet will free up the fly, give it a more natural swim, and catch more fish for you. This is especially true when you're fishing clear water with a slow retrieve.

METHODS FOR STREAMERS

When thinking of streamers as imitations of food forms, there are two bits of behavior worth considering. The first is what the particular form spends most of its time doing. If it's a baitfish, this might be idling about. If it's a dragonfly nymph, then it might be creeping about. The second thing to consider is how the food form might react in the instant it perceives that a hungry trout has suddenly taken to its tail.

A shiner or kokanee might spend most of its time in a school, flitting after insects or plucking at plankters. When a trout chases it, however, one might suppose it uses whatever speed it possesses. A dragonfly nymph, as I'll discuss in its chapter, has a special system for jet propulsion. When a trout enters the territory of its senses, you can expect that the nymph turns on its afterburners.

The same is true of most foods that are imitated by streamers. Even leeches, which have no eyes and seem to grope their way aimlessly most of the time, have sensing systems that pick up aquatic vibrations. I know, because on a recent trip to a remote lake I had to tow a canoe through some leech-infested shallows. Every leech for yards around turned and hurried toward the disturbance I made. It's hard to believe one would fail to be aware of a trout hunting down its track.

Consider these two kinds of movements, then, when choosing a retrieve with a particular streamer. At times you'll want to fish your fly as if it were at idle. But at other times you'll want to fish it as if it's under attack.

Slow Sink and Strip

This method has two parts: the sink and the retrieve.

Trout often take a streamer as it sinks slowly down through the layers of a lake. This is less often true with old-style feather-wings and bucktails, more often true with marabous and other streamers tied with active materials. The reason is simple: As it sinks, the fly looks as if it is swimming toward the bottom. This single factor is an excellent reason to weight your streamers toward the head end rather than balanced in the middle as you would with a nymph. It causes the fly to swim head down, as any natural would do it.

During the sink you have to keep in constant touch with the fly in order to detect a take. That doesn't mean you need a tight line; it would hinder the sink rate. But it does mean you should watch the line tip where it enters the water and be aware of any dart or sudden change in the way it achieves its entry.

The method is excellent in water three to five feet deep, with a long leader and floating line. When the fly has achieved the depth you want, then begin your retrieve. Crawl it back just fast enough to keep in touch with the possibility of a take. Most of the time you'll be fishing by feel. I've seen folks fish this way so attentively that their posture made them look as if they were *listening* for a take.

The slow sink and strip works at a variety of depths, from near the top to the silted bottom. It is especially effective in shallow coves, over woody debris on the bottom, above sparse weed beds that trail up toward the top, or over dense weed beds that lie in shallow water. Use a floating line and a 10- to 12-foot leader, being sure you've stretched all the kinks out of it.

In water five to ten feet deep use the method with a sink-tip line but keep the leader fairly long if the fly is stoutly weighted. When using this method a long tippet that is relatively fine, 3X or 4X, allows the fly to sink more freely than an abrupt and heavy leader.

Rick Hafele used this method to his enjoyment and my embarrassment recently on a little lake above that leech-infested swamp in Canada. I'd portaged the canoe into it the day before, and I thought I had it solved. A Woolly Bugger cast long and retrieved fast had taken lots of fish for me that day. I intended to repeat my

By allowing a streamer to simply sink slowly into the depths, with no action added, Rick Hafele was able to cause lots of trout to come up and dance on the surface of a small Canadian lake.

success on the second day, in front of Rick, but the trout had other intentions.

They ignored my flies for a couple of hours, and I changed frantically from one to another, assuming the problem was color or size or something. While I tried everything I could think of in the stern of the canoe, Rick simply cast his leech off the bow and watched while it sank. Every few minutes something subtle told him to set the hook, and he'd cause another Kamloops rainbow to boil up to the surface.

We could see the white rope leading to our anchor rock about eight feet down in the dark tannic water. A wet-tip line, long leader, and weighted fly were perfect for the situation. I used exactly the same tackle and cast the same fly, but my fast retrieve didn't draw a single strike.

The slow sink and strip is also effective in the profundal depths, especially in midsummer. Use the fastest sinking lines in your system to get the fly down and keep it there. The same countdown method used for fishing a nymph deep will help you

find the depth you want, near the bottom or above the thermocline. You'll need to creep the fly along to keep it where you want
it. A fast retrieve will cause it to ride up toward the surface.

This method has a hidden advantage when fishing deep. Paul
Bech, a British Columbia fisheries biologist, pointed it out to me.
We were fishing a large lake, and he was anchored in his canoe,
fishing above a weed bed, coaxing his fly along so slowly that a
snail would have honked its horn to pass it.

"I don't have to cast as often when I fish it this slow," Paul told
me.

He's right. The slow retrieve, when fishing the depths, lets you
keep your fly down where the fish are a lot longer on each cast.
After you've waited a minute or more for the fly to sink, it seems a
shame to gallop it right back.

Moderate Stripping Retrieve

The most common way to fish a streamer is with absentminded
strips of a foot or so at a time. It is likely that we fall into this
method because it is easy. But it also works a high percentage of
the time. It causes a featherwing or bucktail to swim along like a
fish and a marabou or rabbit-strip dressing to undulate along like a
leech. It imitates the motion of a lot of beasts when they're not
aware of attack.

Before beginning the retrieve you have to give the fly some
time to sink to the level you want to fish it. This is especially true
with a dry line; you have to give the fly a few moments to get
down or it will plane near enough to the surface to leave a wake.
I've seldom had a trout take a fly that was causing a surface wake.

Depth is the first consideration when fishing this way. Even
when fish are holding shallow and are willing to move to the top,
I've taken far more fish with a wet-tip line than I have with a
floater. I can't say whether it's the slight difference in depth – a
matter of inches with a stripping retrieve – or the subdued color of
the wet-tip line. At any rate, the difference is there, and it's usually
best to switch to a sinking or wet-tip line before using the faster
retrieve, even if you're fishing water that's only three feet deep.

When I'm working deeper water, exploring for fish with casts
that expand in an arc around me, I typically fish this retrieve with

a fast-sinking line in my shooting-head system. The depth fished is varied by the countdown method. Once the retrieve starts, the fly will stay on the same level until the end of the running line is reached and the head begins climbing toward the rod.

The moderate strip is a mindless sort of streamer method, and I say that in an affectionate sense. When the casting is going well, it has the same rhythms to it as summer steelheading's step-and-cast, step-and-cast. It gets to be a pleasant repetitive rhythm, occasionally interrupted by the whack of a trout.

The Fast Strip

This is what you do when you want to make your fly look like it's under attack. It is seldom the first option when fishing a streamer, but it is always an important option to consider. Too often we change flies in a constant search for what works, when what we really need to experiment with are the twin factors of depth fished and speed of retrieve.

The fast strip is executed with the same line-hand motion as the moderate strip, only it's done faster, with the line taken in with longer gulps. Many times this retrieve is best used in combination with the slower retrieves, often on the same cast. Race your fly a bit, then rest it, letting it sink. Twitch it up into a teasing retrieve, then speed it up again.

At times trout want the fast retrieve without any change of pace. Don't pause long between strips. Keep the fly moving. I've seen times when trout would follow on a fast strip, then turn away if the retrieve was slowed down.

The fast strip works at all depths. Up near the surface you'll do best using a wet-tip line, although a heavily weighted streamer can be fished on a floating line. An option that has worked well for me is pinching a small shot to the leader just ahead of the hook eye and fishing the streamer on a floater. This gets the fly down quickly and keeps it far enough down so it won't leave a wake. It also has the advantage of causing the fly to dive whenever you pause during the retrieve.

With a wet-tip line you'll still want to use a weighted fly. The extra weight will keep the fly at the same level as the line tip. With full-sink lines, used for exploring the deeper water, weight on the

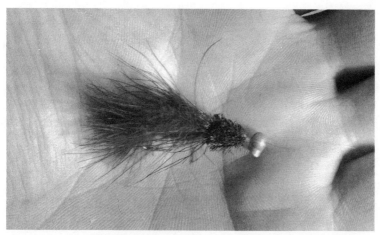

One way to achieve instant depth with a streamer is to pinch a split shot on the leader in front of the hook eye.

fly doesn't make much difference unless you add a lot, which is contrary to the way I fish streamers simply because it makes casting so unpleasant. I'd rather use the line than lead on the fly to determine the depth fished.

A shooting-head or full-sinking-line system, as opposed to wet-belly or wet-head lines, works best with fast retrieves. Lines with floating portions behind the sinking tips tend to draw the fly up toward the surface on a fast retrieve. There's no use wasting all that time you spent counting the fly down if it's just going to fish ten feet at running depth and then plane quickly up toward peri-scope depth.

COVERING THE WATER

Streamer fishing is often exploratory, a way of looking for fish. When it's done along a shoreline, the edge of a drop-off, or along an extended shoal, you want to set up a casting pattern that covers the water thoroughly.

If you're fishing from shore, then you're limited to whatever water you can reach. Cast in an arc around you, starting at one shoreline with a cast almost parallel to the beach, then work your casts outward until you're casting straight toward the center of the

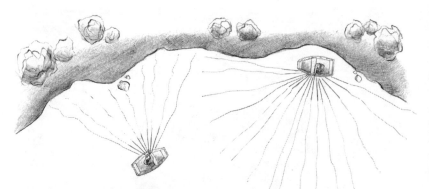

You can fish the shoreline from a boat or float tube in two ways: positioning offshore and casting toward it, or positioning near the shore and casting out away from it.

lake. Continue the arc around until your last cast parallels the opposite shoreline. Then move down the shore until you can cover a new arc of water. If access is limited, move to the next point where you can get a good backcast.

When fishing by boat or float tube there are a couple of ways to set up a casting pattern. The first is to hold just off shore, or off the feature you're fishing, and fire an arc of casts at it from your first position. After you've covered what you can from the first position, move a cast down and cover a new arc. If the wind is blowing, you might have to anchor, pulling up and reanchoring at each new position.

The second way to cover water is by positioning the boat or tube as close as you can to shore, then fanning your casts around in an arc the same way you'd do it from shore. It's surprising to me the number of times I've done this and suddenly have taken fish that wouldn't come to a fly retrieved in the opposite direction, away from the shoreline. I can't explain it except in theoretical terms. Fish might be expecting their meals to swim toward shore, not away from it.

This last method seems most effective when fishing a drop-off that's removed from the shoreline. Anchor on the shallow side and make your casts out over the deep water. Let the fly sink, then retrieve it toward the drop, angling up out of the depths.

12

Trolling and Wind-drifting

Occasional boils welled up around the lake, but the rises were so scattered it would have been a waste of time to chase them. I launched the tube anyway and flippered out through the weedy shoreline shallows. My fins kicked up clouds of turbulence; each cloud had a couple of strange bright green arrows drawn through it. I slowed down, made a strong kick, then leaned over the bow to peer closely into the water.

The arrows were olive damselfly nymphs, dislodged and tossed up in the turbulence, regaining their grip on the water, then darting in straight lines back toward the sanctuary of the weeds. Most of them were small. But some were large enough to be imitated with a #10 fly tied on a long-shank hook.

I didn't relate the rare boils out in the lake to the damsels in the shallows, but I did suspect a trout would see an odd damsel in its migrations around the lake. So I selected an olive damsel pattern, tied it to the tippet, took one long cast, and flippered off at a slow troll.

I didn't catch many fish that day—only four. Another fellow

caught two fishing midge pupae all day. Nobody else caught any, and there were lots of other people trying. Four fish felt awfully good that day, especially given the size of the thumps they caused. They averaged around 3 pounds.

Trolling with fly-fishing gear is often regarded not to be fly-fishing. Some folks frown on it. I'm a firm believer in trolling as a way to explore a lake, and also as a way to enjoy a lake. Trolling is often the catalyst that lets me find fish and figure out what they are taking.

Trolling can help you solve the mystery of a lake.

ARMING YOURSELF

Proper equipment for trolling obviously starts with something to get you around. It can be any of the aquatic transportation types described in the earlier chapter on that subject. Float tubes are excellent; any kind of boat will work. I like my pram, and I stroke it slowly around lots of lakes, towing a fly, until I find signs that something else will work better. Trolling is a great way to fish from a canoe because they are so graceful when moving, so cranky when still.

Cartoppers are fine, although I have some quarrels with aluminum. It's almost impossible to dampen the oarlocks so you can row without clattering and clanking. Use Teflon oarlock wells and rubber oar buttons to subdue some of it. You would be surprised at the number of trout that turn away from your boat without ever telling you about it. You'll only know the difference if you find a way to silence your aluminum boat or make the switch to fiber-glass or wood.

Trailerable boats work well for trolling given that you either have oars or an electric motor to make them move. A gas motor makes quite a commotion under the water and vibrates the entire boat. Recall that trout have a lateral line to sense low-frequency vibrations. Trout can be caught using a motor, but it reduces your chances significantly, envelops you in a cloud of noise and smoke, and to me at least, pushes you toward the edges of the definitions of fly-fishing. But then others think I'm already over the edge by mentioning trolling at all. You have to decide for yourself where the borders exist, if there are any.

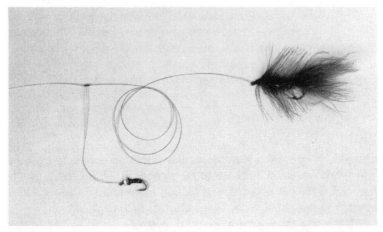

When exploring a lake by trolling or casting, it helps to offer the trout a choice, in this case a Woolly Bugger and a smaller TDC. *Jim Schollmeyer*

Whatever kind of boat you use, do your best to rig it for silent running. Even my wooden pram put quite a few fish off their feed before I switched from plastic to rubber buttons on the oars.

Fishing gear isn't any different than you'd use if you were casting. If fish are feeding very near the top, a dry line will do. Otherwise it's best to use at least a wet tip. Most of the time I prefer my system rod with a fast-sinking shooting head.

Fly selection should be based on what you know or guess about the predominant trout food forms in the lake. Generally you'll want to consider imitations, or at least suggestions, of damselfly or dragonfly nymphs, leeches, or crustaceans and the types of smaller nymphs that have the capacity to swim. Cryptic insect types are not the best candidates on which to model trolling flies.

In addition, your selection should be based on some sort of internal action the fly might produce. Wet flies, nymphs, and streamers that have some fibrous, working parts are always best. Marabou is an obvious first choice. I use a lot of soft-hackled wet flies with weepy hackles that open and close with the patient rowing motion.

Most of the time I like to troll with a couple of flies on the leader. The point fly will be a streamer, usually a Woolly Bugger in about a #10, olive or black. The dropper is usually a nymph or soft-hackle. About half the time it's a #14 TDC, a midge pupa imitation. The two-fly cast gives trout a choice. I've also heard it speculated that a streamer behind a small nymph makes it look like something big is chasing something small. It makes sense to me, although I haven't been able to penetrate that far into the way a trout puzzles things out.

PROPER POSTURE

The first thing to do is to get some line out. It should be more than you think you need, with 45 to 60 feet of line about right. Much less and you'll get fewer strikes. Much more and you'll lose some control and not hook as many of the strikes that you do get.

You can either cast the line out or simply drop the fly to the water and row away from it. They both work. I usually make a short cast, shake more line onto the water, then move away from the fly until I have it out the distance I want it. If you do choose to cast, and you're using two flies on the leader, be sure they don't get into a quarrel. I don't know how often I've flippered or rowed around a lake for half an hour, then pulled my flies in for a check only to discover that they're tangled and I haven't been fishing.

It's also a good idea to draw the fly in once in a while for a physical exam, to be sure it's not carrying crud. A dangle of weed will turn fish away. I don't recall ever catching a trout when my fly was fouled.

Once the line is out, prop the rod at an angle that will best hook fish. Usually that means the lowest angle you can get it to the water. If you're tubing, hold the rod and aim it right at the point where the line lies on the water. It doesn't hurt to hold the rod tip underwater if you're using a sinking line.

If you have to prop the rod over a gunwale or transom, then do what you can to lower the angle of the rod tip. If it's propped at a 45-degree angle to the line, you're going to miss most strikes and have a dandy time playing those you do hook because of all the slack in the line.

In my pram I'm able to lay the butt of the rod on the rowing seat with the tip over the transom. The rod is only at a slight angle upward, and a strike comes quickly against weight, which sets the hook. I suppose a big fish could yank the rod out of the boat, but it would probably be worth seeing it happen. So far I've always managed to get to the rod before it does anything more than fall off the seat.

There is an exception to the rule of pointing the rod at the line entry. If you expect to catch large trout that hit with a thump, then the angle should be steeper to give the fish a chance to tug against the bend of the rod. I did it that way the day I trolled a damsel around the lake and caught four fish. I knew the lake held large fish and that they were bold fighters. So I fastened the rod straight across the float tube and clamped it into its Velcro holders.

Its posture was then at a 90-degree angle to the line, which I would never do when after small fish. Those trout, however, were so eager that they set the hook themselves and then set the rod to dancing.

I am infatuated with that instant in which the untended rod suddenly begins to dance.

Always place the rod where you can reach it quickly without having to reach around anything. If you are in a rowboat, have your oars tied in or pinned in so that you can drop them when you have a hit without watching them flop out of the oarlocks and float away. That's distressing, especially when you're playing a big trout.

At the first sign of a hit pick the rod up as quickly as you can, with a slow and even lift. Don't yank it upward. If the trout is big and going the other way, you'll feel a jerk, and think you are one.

READING THE WATER

If trolling is largely exploring, then you should aim to cover any features you suspect might hold trout. That includes the shoreline and any adjacent features such as drop-offs, rocky points, shallow weed beds, or deposits of woody debris. Shoals away from the shoreline are good producers; sometimes you'll find them by getting your trolled fly snagged up on them, down in depths you can't see. If that happens, fiddle around in the area, adjust your depth, and see if you can find some fish.

Deep weed beds are obvious hotspots for trolling as well as casting. If, in your trolling, you suddenly come into an area where you're hanging up on weeds, you might want to anchor and cast in the area for a while, using your fly to probe it.

When trolling, keep your rod at a low angle to the water unless you expect large trout. This photo shows the angle of my dad's rod at the instant of a hit.

But don't limit trolling to features you can see or those you suspect. Cover some lake. Look for features worth fishing. But let your fly do some looking for you, too. If you bump into fish, then mark the area and traverse it again. I had something happen last season that I still can't explain – and I suspect I never will.

I was trolling a small lake, less than ten acres, with a very scattered fall population of trout that are fat. I'd been at it for two hours, idling along in my pram, just taking a stroke at the oars now and then to bump the boat forward. I'd covered the shallows, then the depths, and had gotten to the point where I figured I'd have to cross a submerged spring by accident if I was going to stir any trout. Then I spotted a canoe paddle lost on shore, so I turned the boat toward it. It was time to get out, tinkle, and stretch. And I could use that paddle.

Just before I got to shore, my rod went into its dance.

After I netted the fish I rowed briskly back to where I'd been when I spotted the paddle. Then I rowed slowly right toward it again. Just before I got to shore, my rod danced again.

That was it. I tried it again and again. I aimed at the same spot from a thousand different directions, crossed it going north and south, east and west. I got only the two fish—plus a big load of superstition. When I fish the same lake, I still follow that same pattern. A psychologist watching me fish would probably make some notes about compulsions. I even left that paddle there to aim at, although somebody else came along and lifted it later.

I still suspect there's a spring down there and that it was no accident that I encountered those two trout when doing exactly the same thing in the same place. But it hasn't worked since.

Explore various depths. There are three ways to do it. You can vary the weight on the fly, the sink rate of the line, or the speed at which you troll. Switch flies from time to time, although once you've used a fly enough to gain some confidence in it, it's best to be patient with it. Don't get to switching every five minutes unless something tells you it would be wise to do so.

But do make changes from time to time. Recall the three major variables: fly pattern, depth fished, and speed of retrieve. Work with them each in turn. If nothing else, it will give you something to think about.

Trolling speed should be tied in part to the natural you're imitating. Don't gallop a dragonfly nymph. Try a leech both fast and slow. Speed also should be tied to the depth you want to fish. If you want your line to drop farther down, slow yourself down, and you'll fish deeper.

Your trolling speed also should be tied to the speed at which you want to enjoy the lake. If you're out for exercise, tie on a featherwing or bucktail streamer and lay into the oars. If you're

The day was so bad the wind would normally have stopped us, but by wind-drifting Jim Schollmeyer was able to hold a beautiful trout in his hands.

out for the scenery and some surprise, take your time; take a single stroke now and then.

I've found that the slower I troll, the faster I get the kind of surprises I like.

WIND-DRIFTING

Wind-drifting is how you troll when the wind is blowing so hard you can't do much else. But that's not all there is to it. You can wind-drift and cast, too.

When you're trolling, just let the wind become your propellant. Use the angle of the boat to the wind, or the direction you take if you're tubing, to determine how fast you let the wind push you. Row or paddle against it to fish slow. Let it push you if you want to fish fast. All other factors remain the same as they would be if you were huffing yourself along without the wind.

When you want to wind-drift and cast, it becomes a slightly different story. There are times when the wind is so fierce that it's the only story around.

Jim Schollmeyer and I fished Oregon's giant and windblown Crane Prairie Reservoir one day in early spring. A cold wind whipped off the Cascade Mountains, and there wasn't much we could do to control the boat, even though it was a fancy guide model with pedestal seats and a trolling motor. We tried, but finally gave up and set the boat adrift down an old river channel. Then we sat at bow and stern and cast streamers with the wind. We had only one strike. Jim's rainbow weighed 6 pounds.

Sometimes you can set up an angle of drift that takes you right along the cover you want to fish, as Jim and I were able to do down that river channel. More often the wind is contrary and takes you where it will, or it forces you to constantly fight it to keep out of trouble and onto water you want to fish. Try to make some peace with it and fish as well as you can.

Be sure to make peace in a way that lets you cast without risk. If there are two people in the boat, it might be best to switch off; one can troll while the other casts. It's a great way to explore the water in a couple of different ways while keeping hooks out of ears.

You can wind-drift with any fly type and line-sink rate you'd use with any other method. In Britain they have worked out elaborate systems for fishing a dry on a dropper above a couple of wets or nymphs that work as sea anchors, keeping the cast drifting along and working right. I haven't worked with those systems, preferring to stick to one-fly casts when the wind is blowing, but I don't see why they wouldn't work here as well as they do there.

13

Sight Fishing

I fished a still sunrise with a couple of friends from my home club recently. They were relatively new to fly-fishing, and the lake treated them roughly. It was shallow around its edges, its water was clear as air, and everything was starkly lit for about one hundred feet out. The bottom, only a foot or two down, was a dense crewcut of weeds.

The rainbows that cruised above those weeds were big enough to give a beginner slight tremors. They moved slowly, confidently, in loose-knit schools of ten to fifteen fish, startling insects up out of the vegetation, chasing them down with swift darts punctuated by quick body twists at the take. It was beautiful to watch. But my friends didn't spend enough time watching it.

They waded right in and began casting, and in three hours of morning they hooked one fish each.

Some things were wrong that cost them lots of opportunities. First, they were wading in the water the fish wanted to cruise, displacing them into deeper water where the trout were less satisfied and where it was harder to see them. Second, their move-

Sight fishing requires a calm day, clear and shallow water, and cruising fish.

ments were so constant that wading waves extended to the edge of casting range. If you're sight fishing and you can't cast beyond your wading waves, you're not sight fishing.

Some things were also wrong when they got opportunities. Their rods were long and soft and heavy, too slow to deliver crisp but delicate presentations. Their lines were 6- and 7-weights, not light enough. Their leaders were 8 or 9 feet long, and tapered to about 4X: neither long enough nor fine enough. Their flies were #6 streamers, which work on this lake most of the time but not when trout feed on insects that are #16 and smaller.

I point all this out because most of the time I'm at the other end of the lesson: getting the educated finger wagged at me. On this occasion I sat and watched the trout awhile, then rigged out with a leader 15 feet long, fined down to 4 feet of 6X tippet. I slipped just to the edge of some reeds, then stood as still as a reed myself.

When a pod of trout moved into the periphery of my vision, I tilted my rod far to the side and flicked a cast that was little longer than the leader itself, placing the fly several feet ahead of the fish. The #18 nymph made a tiny splat and slowly sank. When a trout swam near the fly, I lifted the rod to prod it slightly. There was a quick dart and turn. I raised the rod and caused a detonation.

In the next three hours I educated about a dozen trout. But I was not able to pat myself on the back for holding many of them in my hands. The weeds, combined with the fragile tippet, caused lots of early partings.

Sight fishing has three essential parts: the approach to the situation, presentation of the fly, and detection of a take.

THE APPROACH

You have to be like the heron. Trout cruising visibly are always wary of predation, all of their senses are turned up, and they're always ready to bolt. You want to move into position to intercept a pod, or a cruising individual, but you don't want to chase visible trout. You'll never catch up. Let them come to you.

Wear subdued clothing that blends with the background. A bright hat, vest, and shirt become flags, although if you don't wave them it's surprising how little they disturb trout. Movement is the key that causes trout to telescope their focus outward onto you.

Don't make any quick moves with your arms, head, or fly rod. When you move into position, or if you have to relocate, advance your legs slowly to keep wading waves slight. Once you're where you want to be, wait for all the waves to subside. Then refrain from moving your body and legs in a way that makes more waves. Kneel if you can, or crouch to keep your profile low. Tilt your rod to the side on the cast to keep it out of the cone of vision of the trout.

Your equipment is part of the approach. If the light is right, wear polarized sunglasses. I like flip-ups because I wear glasses, and it often happens that I can look to the right and see better with them, to the left and see better without them, according to the angle of the sun. I always carry miniature binoculars, although I use them most often for watching birds and spying on more successful anglers. But they can help a lot when sight fishing, mostly for the scouting you do while watching from the bank and trying to decide how to make your approach.

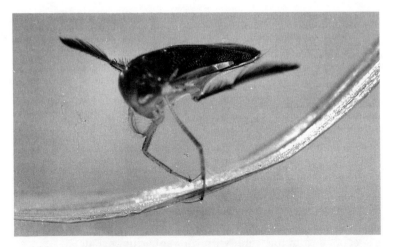

Most of the time when trout feed visibly in the shallows, they're nosing such insects as this water boatman out of the weed beds. You can fool them with exact imitations like this one, or just as often with dressings that are simply rough approximations. *Jim Schollmeyer*

Your line should be floating and light, 5-weight or less. Since sight fishing is almost always done during windless conditions – wind waves make it impossible to see into the water – you can get away nicely with a 2- or 3-weight. The rod should be delicate enough to load with very little line beyond its tip but crisp enough to turn over a long leader. The leader should be 12 to 15 feet long, with a tippet that is balanced to the size of the fly and makes up 3 to 5 feet of the leader.

Be sure to stretch all kinks out of the leader. It has to lie out straight; there's no use casting a 15-foot leader if it's going to shrink to half its length. If you're forced to fish small and subsurface in water that is less than a couple of feet deep, which is almost the rule in sight fishing, then grease the leader down to about a foot from the point.

If fish are feeding on top, the fly at the point should be a dry that matches the hatch. Often the victims will be midges or tiny terrestrials stuck and struggling feebly in the surface film. You have to snoop around with your nose close to the water. Try to lift a specimen from the water with your aquarium net and get a close look at it. Do your best to match it in size and shape; worry about color if your fly boxes give you that luxury.

If the fish are feeding on large subaqueous creatures such as dragonfly nymphs or leeches, then use appropriate streamers. The fish will be very aggressive in their behavior; you'll almost be afraid to enter the water.

Most of the time visibly cruising trout nose around in the shallows prying mayfly nymphs, water boatmen, midge larvae, and scuds out of weed beds. The best imitations are tiny nymphs, #14 through #20. It's surprising how often you'll solve the situation once you choose a nymph that's approximately the right size and then fish it at the right depth without worrying about matching anything else. The amount of weight on the fly is the key.

For sight fishing you have to have some nymphs that are modestly weighted so they'll sink fairly quickly in front of a sighted fish. But you also have to have others that are not weighted at all so you can cast them ahead of a fish and let them sink inches at a time, and not very deep, as the fish slowly approaches.

I don't recommend tying special flies for this kind of fishing. Most of the time you'll be basing your fly selection on some sort of food form. A study of Part 3, Lake Food Forms and Their Imitations, should be your guide there. Most of the time you'll already own the flies you need for sight fishing.

PRESENTATION

Enticing the take is the second of the three parts to sight fishing. You'll be fishing to trout that you have spotted and that you can watch.

Many times you will want to cast the fly to one end of the area they're cruising while they are at the other. This lets you get the fly out there without spooking them. After the cast you return to your heronlike posture, and the fly sits if it's a dry or sinks if it's a nymph, ready to entice the trout when they return.

When the fly is already in position, usually on or near the bottom, then you can activate it with a tiny twitch, or a lifting movement, when you feel an approaching fish is close enough to notice it. If the bottom is muddy, the tiny tuft of silt the fly kicks up will help sell it. If the bottom is clean, movement alone will usually be coaxing enough. But don't overdo it. A slow lifting of the rod is sometimes too much. A hand-twist retrieve, beginning at the right moment, is often better. You'll seldom want to cause the fly to move with any urgency, although it's tempting to yank it up where the trout can encounter it.

Most times you'll watch the water with the fly in your hand, poised to cast, with the leader and some line beyond the rod tip. When a fish is sighted, place the fly several feet ahead of its path, far enough that it won't notice the flash of the line or leader in the air. If the fish approaches at an angle toward you, then place the fly close enough that the pip of its landing is visible to the fish. Unless you're casting depth charges, the tiny entry itself acts as an enticement.

As the fish continues to approach a nymph, merely let it sink. Lots of times the trout will take it on the drop. That is the first presentation to try—just as the dead drift is always the first way to fool fish when fishing a stream—with an activated fly always second. In sight fishing stillwaters, begin to move the fly if you feel the fish has seen it but chooses to ignore it, or if you think the fish fails to notice the fly. A tiny twitch or hand-twist will get it moving and will attract the trout's attention for a take, or a snub.

The worst angle of presentation is to a trout moving straight away from you, or at any acute angle that points its tail toward you. Then you have to cross it with the leader, if not the line, to get

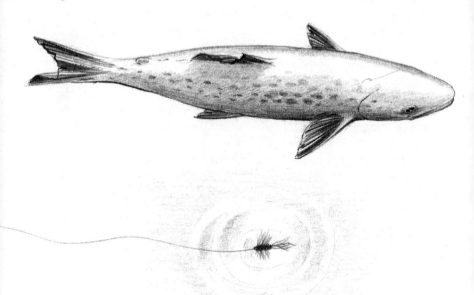

When a trout swims straight away from you, try setting the fly onto the water to the side and slightly behind its line of sight, hard enough to attract its attention.

the fly ahead of it. Instead, try pipping the fly to the water about three feet to one side or the other, even slightly behind. The idea is to attract the trout's notice with the entry of the fly without startling it with the flash of the leader. It will often turn to the take.

A trout swimming at a 90-degree angle across your bow, or some approximation of that angle, is a lot easier. If you've spotted it soon enough, you can cast far enough ahead of it to intercept its path. The trout will move to the fly on the drop, or you can use movement to coax it.

The best situation of all is a trout swimming straight toward you, given that you can make a cast before it's so close that you don't dare move, which abruptly turns it into the worst situation of all. When a trout moves in a direct line toward the rod, the cast will place the fly ahead of the leader and line, and the fly is almost sure to be all the trout is able to see. I have found that such fish can almost always be teased into a take unless the fly is far wrong.

DETECTING TAKES

This last of the three parts of sight fishing can sometimes be the most difficult. And it's always the most frustrating when you fail to get the hook home, because you know you've executed all the other parts right and you deserve the reward of the dancing trout. However, there's a rule in fly-fishing that the fish that's not hooked doesn't fight very well.

In sight fishing you'll rarely feel the take. You have to become aware of it in some other manner. Sometimes you'll actually see the take, with the fly in sight and the trout's mouth opening and closing whitely and the fly suddenly gone. That's the ultimate, and you deserve congratulations if you can wait to set the hook until after the trout has closed down on the fly. I won't tell you about the incantations I've devised for the times I've jerked a fly away from a fish. You can make up your own.

Most of the time you'll have to detect some hint of the take that is not a direct report of it. This might be a mere turn of the trout when it's in the area you know is inhabited by your fly. If the trout approaches the fly and then turns and swims away, raise the rod slowly. Often it looks like a refusal, but the fly is buttoned right where you want it, and you come up against weight, which surprises you as well as the trout.

If you see the white flash of the trout's mouth, that's likely the exact news you want. Set the hook.

If you see the line tip twitch, the fish is already on—but it's also already about to be off. Raise the rod, but not abruptly because the trout might be swimming in the other direction, and you'll pop the tippet.

The most likely sign is some slight change in the way the leader point enters the water above the fly. It might draw down, or it might simply cease to sink. Whatever it does that is different from what it was doing before, set the hook.

A sharp hook is critical in sight fishing. It increases the chance that the trout will hook itself, or at least hold on to the hook until you have a chance to set it. The hook set should be initiated with a soft upward lift of the rod, drawing the hook home if the trout holds it. You'll be fishing fine; an abrupt hook set would break you off, especially if your rod is stiff. The subtle set will get the small hook into the trout's lip where you want it. And if the trout has by chance not taken the fly, and you've made a mistake, you won't compound it by jerking the fly out of there and ripping the line off the water.

That will startle the trout, which in its fright will send the rest of the pod flying out of sight.

Part III
Lake Food Forms and Their Imitations

14

When Trout Feed

I'm lazy on lakes. If the trip is to be longer than a day's duration, I try to see the whole day in order to discover a time when fish are active and feeding. But I often take time off in the absence of visible activity to read a book or nose around in the shallows. These peripheral activities are most valuable in midsummer, when the days are long and the trout are less likely to be moved during the warmest hours. If I try to pound it out all day every day, especially on a long trip, it's easy to get worn out.

However, trout activity is not always visible. Evidence of feeding gets sent to the surface a lot less than half the time. So I always spend at least a few hours during each day exploring likely cover, or the shallows, or the depths, depending on signals the water sends and the time of year.

This combination of laziness and inquisitiveness works well for me, although I know more successful fishermen who can cast from dawn to dusk without letup. They always have the trout in danger because they always have a fly in the water.

A good friend once confessed annoyance with me because I

lay back in the boat and took a snooze for an hour while he kept fishing. He caught no fish during that period, which was what I suspected would happen, and was why I snoozed. It was mid-summer and midday, and my friend might have happened into a pod of cruising fish and made me look foolish. But I chose to conserve some energy to expend in the afternoon and evening, when activity could be expected to pick up slightly. It did, and we both caught fish then.

It was a knowledge of the major food forms present that gave me a chance to take some time off. I knew damselfly nymphs would begin moving in late afternoon for an early-evening emergence. Knowing when to take a nap is not the major benefit of such study, but to me it's an important one.

The most important benefit lies in the fish you can fool if you know what they eat.

I've mentioned, and repeated, the three major variables in stillwater fly-fishing: the fly chosen, the depth at which it is fished, and the speed at which it is retrieved. All three are best based on knowledge of food forms that trout eat. When you're doing that, you are suddenly showing trout something they've at least seen lately, and have likely eaten.

If trout feed selectively, and you fail to recognize and respond to the situation, then you're not likely to fool any fish at all. Paul Bech pointed this out to me recently by taking several fish from a little lake that didn't supply any to me.

Leeches were the primary suspect in the lake. I tried an Olive Woolly Bugger for an hour or so, then a black one, and followed with a litany of attempts based on other food forms. Nothing struck the trout's fancy. But Paul came along a little later in his own canoe, fished a Blood Leech based on his superior knowledge of the foods that live in the lakes of his home province, British Columbia, and found the fish foolishly easy. The leeches in the lake were reddish brown. A pattern in the right color turned out to be deadly.

Recognition of the food forms that trout eat helps you select flies that match them in size, form, and as Paul proved, color. But the rewards of recognition go far beyond fly selection. When you understand a food's habitat, then you know the kind of water where its imitation will work best. And you also know the right depth at which to fish it. When you understand the food's behavior – the way it moves in the water – then you'll know the right speed to retrieve the fly you fish for it.

Collecting and observation play important roles in understanding aquatic insect behavior as well as the behavior of other beasts. I put in a stint of several years during which I carried a long-handled specimen net at all times. I used it often, sweeping it through weed beds in the shallows, reaching down until my elbow and sometimes even my shoulder got soaked, to poke at the bottom and see what might live there. I never killed a dinner fish without examining its stomach. I still don't. I have, however, slipped to carrying a tiny aquarium net with which I can pluck an occasional specimen off the surface.

I would recommend that you develop a similar curiosity and spend at least some time snooping around, learning about the things that live in lakes and that get eaten by trout. It will increase your knowledge of the trout's world. Anything that increases your knowledge about trout also improves your chances of catching them.

To fuel your curiosity, make up a net by lashing a kitchen strainer to an old broom handle, or devise a similar means of extending it into the depths. Dip it into all of the different environments that you can find in the waters you fish. You'll soon see that what lives in one place is replaced by something else in another. You'll also soon collect and observe most of the food forms listed in the later chapters in this book. Once you've collected them, they will suddenly become a part of what you know, not just what you've read about.

If you've never gone out and collected before, what you suddenly see will astonish you.

15

Mayflies

Mayflies in stillwater find a narrower range of niches than they do in streams. They exist in a more restricted variety. The most important species belong to the swimmer category, their nymphs moving about agilely and sometimes swiftly. The burrowers are represented by scattered populations of *Hexagenia*, the largest mayfly and therefore one of great importance wherever you do happen to find it. The crawlers sponsor hatches of tiny *Caenis*.

Trout are not often found feeding selectively on these smaller populations. But, like all things that trout eat, they become suddenly and alarmingly important whenever great numbers of them get concentrated into a specific area at a certain time, causing trout to disdain all else.

CALLIBAETIS

Callibaetis are by far the most important of the stillwater mayflies. Their hatches are heavy in waters from the East to the West. They are found in almost all lakes and ponds. Their numbers are almost

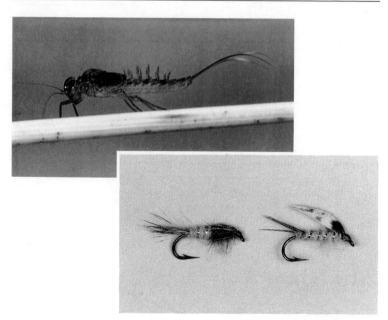

The *Callibaetis* nymph is a bold and active swimmer. It can be imitated
with the standard Gold Ribbed Hare's Ear nymph or with a Hare's Ear
wet fly. *Jim Schollmeyer*

always great enough to cause selective feeding when a hatch
happens. They have two or three broods in a single year: one
in spring, a second in midsummer, and in most waters a third in
fall. Their hatches are spread out over a long period of time,
prompting trout to feed on them more days than they don't during
the fishing season.

This group provides opportunities in all three of the life stages
of the mayfly: nymph, dun, and spinner.

Nymph

The *Callibaetis* nymph has three tails fringed with hairs that effec-
tively broaden the tails and make them better swimming paddles
in the water. The two antennae are long, in contrast to the only
other important group with which they can be confused in lakes
and ponds, the *Siphlonurus* mayflies. Some of the forward leaflike

gill structures arrayed on the abdominal segments have tiny re-
curved flaps. Nymphs range from #12 to #16, with the larger specimens usually found during spring hatches and the smallest in fall.
Colors range from tannish brown to bright green and always blend
with the bottom or vegetation types on which they live.

Imitations of *Callibaetis* nymphs should be long and slender,
usually tied on hooks that are 1X or 2X long. Depending on the
color of the nymph, I have found that either a standard or an olive
Gold-Ribbed Hare's Ear, tied slender and with slight weight, works
well for them.

Gold-Ribbed Hare's Ear

Hook: 1X or 2X long-shank #12 to #16

Thread: Tan or olive

Weight: 6 to 10 turns of lead wire

Tail: Hare's mask guard hairs

Rib: Narrow gold tinsel

Body: Natural or olive hare's mask fur

Wingcase: Brown or olive-dyed turkey

Thorax: Natural dark hare's mask, or dyed olive

I also have had good success fishing either a standard Hare's
Ear Wet fly, or an olive version, when *Callibaetis* nymphs are
active.

Hare's Ear Wet

Hook: Standard dry fly, #12 to #16

Thread: Tan or olive

Tail: 2 to 3 pheasant tail fibers

Rib: Narrow gold tinsel

Body: Natural or olive hare's mask

Wing: Hen pheasant quill

Callibaetis **duns are the most common mayfly hatch on stillwaters. They should be matched with simple Compara-dun dressings that present accurate silhouettes of the natural on the water.** *Jim Schollmeyer*

Hatches typically take place in April and May, again in June or July, with a final hatch coming off in most waters in September and early October. Each hatch has a distinct peak, with insect numbers building up toward it and then dwindling down to a few sporadic individuals coming off daily in the period between hatches. Nymphs are most active, and therefore available to trout, in the prehatch period, usually between 9:00 A.M. and noon.

Nymph habitat is anywhere that the insects find periphyton fields to browse on. As always, they are regulated by the limits of light. The largest numbers will be found in weed beds. But scattered populations will flit along the bottom if food and oxygen are abundant down there. The nymphs are often found far from shore in lakes that are less than twenty feet deep, if there is vegetation growth down in the depths.

Because the naturals are fast and agile swimmers, *Callibaetis* nymph imitations should be fished with an active retrieve. A moderate stripping retrieve works best, but give the fly an occasional pause, mimicking the resting nymph.

Dun

Callibaetis duns have two tails and mottled wings. They run a narrow color range from tan to olive and more rarely gray. Almost all species have at least some olive on the underside of the abdomen, which is the side trout see and the one you should imitate. They range from #12 down to #16.

I have found that the best imitations are tied in styles that show a good silhouette to the trout. Since flotation is not a problem on lakes, you can usually dispense with hackles. At one time I tied all of my *Callibaetis* dun and spinner patterns on 3X or 4X fine-wire hooks. But trout in lakes often run large, and I've had too many light hooks straighten out to take such chances again.

Callibaetis Compara-dun

Hook: Standard dry fly, #12 to #16

Thread: Olive

Wing: Natural light tan deer hair

Tails: Tan Micro Fibettes

Body: Tannish olive fur or synthetic

Though the *Callibaetis* Compara-dun is the pattern I use most often during these hatches, thorax ties also work well, as will any mayfly dun style that lowers the body of the fly tight to the water. The above dressing is representative; you'll want to collect specimens on your own waters and vary the colors to match exactly what you find.

The spent *Callibaetis* spinner is difficult to see on the water, but is very important to the fisherman. Its imitation can be as simple as an Adams Midge with hackles trimmed on the bottom. *Jim Schollmeyer*

Spring hatches typically start when the water is warmest, between noon and 2:00 P.M., or even 3:00 P.M., and last two to three hours. Midsummer hatches tend to move into the earlier hours, starting around 10:00 A.M. or even earlier and lasting into early afternoon. Fall hatches move back toward the warmest part of the day. At any time of year an overcast day tends to prolong the hatch, sometimes for several hours.

The duns usually sit still on the water for a few seconds, then fly away. Your imitation should be cast to feeding trout and allowed to simply sit. If the weather is windy or rainy, the natural's first attempts at flight sometimes fail, and a twitched fly will often

attract the attention of cruising trout. But don't overdo it; give the
fly some slight movement, then let it rest again.

Spinner

At one time I wrote that *Callibaetis* spinner falls are not important.
The trout have proved my error on that one time after time. Now
that I know they are important, I still have trouble solving them at
times.

The spinners have two tails. The wings are usually clear in the
males and mottled in the females. Body color ranges from tannish
brown to slate gray, with the latter color most common. Size varies
from #14 down to #18, again with the largest specimens appearing
early in the season, the smallest as the season winds down.

I often cut the wings and bottom hackles off an Adams in the
appropriate size to match *Callibaetis* spinner falls. Sometimes it
works, sometimes it doesn't. The one dressing that has taken fish
for me most consistently during their dances is the Adams Midge
with a V-notch cut in its hackles. As with the dun, I once tied these
on extra-fine hooks, but I now tie them all on standard dry-fly
hooks to hold heavy trout.

Adams Midge

Hook: Standard dry fly, #14 to #18

Thread: Black

Tail: Grizzly hackle fibers

Body: Muskrat fur

Hackle: Grizzly, wound full, then cut out on
bottom

This pattern has solved some *Callibaetis* spinner falls for me. It
has failed in others. But I haven't come up with a dressing that
works any better. I suspect solutions to sticky situations might lie
in the realm of color variations rather than a dressing that is more
complicated. The simplicity of this tie appeals to me.

Spinners usually come out to dance in the sunshine in late

The *Siphlonurus* nymph is a swimmer, like the *Callibaetis*, but has shorter antennae and is usually larger and more robust. Its imitation should be tied on a long shank hook, like this Near Enough by Polly Rosborough. *Jim Schollmeyer*

afternoon, after the day's dun hatch is over. Because they await flight in shoreline vegetation, their return is always associated with the shoreline, although at times they move far out over the open water. But most spinner fishing will be near shore. Exhausted naturals fall to the water with their wings either upright or spent. They do not always expire without a struggle, and a fly that is left to sit for a while, then twitched to attract attention, often draws up a brutal strike out of all proportion to the size of the insect that incites it.

SIPHLONURUS

Siphlonurus are not important in all stillwaters. But lakes that have populations of them tend to have them in large numbers, and therefore the hatches are very important when they happen.

Nymph

Siphlonurus nymphs have three fringed tails and large gills that are doubled on the first two abdominal segments. Their short antennae are the most distinct feature separating them from *Callibaetis*. They are typically larger, #10 or #12. Typical colors are light to dark gray, with some species light tan to pale yellow. They have a single generation each season, and their hatch period is limited, not spread through the entire season.

Imitations of these large nymphs should be fairly close to the naturals. I have found Polly Rosborough's Near Enough, detailed in his book *Tying and Fishing the Fuzzy Nymphs*, the best style. Its size and color can be changed slightly to match any variation you might find on your own home waters.

Near Enough

Hook: 2X or 3X long, #10 to #12

Thread: Tan

Tail: Mallard flank fibers, dyed tan

Body: Gray fox fur

Legs: Mallard flank fibers, dyed tan

Wing case: Butts of leg fibers

Because these hatches come off in spring and early summer, the nymphs are most important as they approach mature size, early in the fishing season. They migrate to shore, where they crawl out for actual emergence, so waters right at the edges are best when nymphs are most active. That is why they are tied without weight. Early in the season, before the migration for emergence, the naturals flit about in weed beds and along the bottom wherever light strikes and periphyton grows.

Siphlonurus nymphs are brisk and agile swimmers. Your presentation should consist of fast strips with an occasional pause, to represent a nymph that is alternately swimming and resting.

Dun

Siphlonurus duns have two tails. Their wings are not mottled. Both bodies and wings are usually grayish in color, although a few are tannish yellow. They are #10 to #12.

Because the nymphs migrate to shore and crawl out on reed stems or similar objects before the dun emerges, the dun stage is not as important as the nymph. But duns are often blown to the water on blustery days, and an imitation will then fool some fish.

Siphlonurus duns are not found on the water very often. When they are, they can be imitated with dressings such as the Gray Wulff. *Jim Schollmeyer*

You could construct an exact imitation, but on these sorts of days an Adams or Gray Wulff will often work just fine.

Gray Wulff

Hook: Standard dry fly, #10 to #12

Thread: Gray

Wings: Natural dun deer hair, split

Tail: Deer hair

Body: Muskrat fur

Hackle: Blue dun

The hatch typically happens between early April and mid-June. Duns often emerge at night, but will come out in late afternoon if the sky is densely overcast. A few specimens always seem to emerge in open water near the shoreline, although most crawl out of the water before emergence. The duns are usually quiescent on the water until they are able to fly away. But during blustery weather they make attempts at flight that often fail, and a fly that is twitched can take trout.

Spinner

Siphlonurus spinners have two tails, clear wings, and are a dark wine to an almost blackish gray color. They are large for mayflies, #10 to #12. I have not personally encountered a fishable spinner fall on lakes, although I have on streams. I won't offer a dressing here, but recommend that you try an appropriate Comparaspinner dressing if you encounter a fall and collect a specimen. The dressing will have split tails, a dubbed body, and a hackle that is wound full, then clipped on top and bottom.

HEXAGENIA

These are the largest mayflies, with duns over an inch long. Their imitations should be tied on #8 or even #6 hooks.

Hexagenia **nymphs are big characters, with beautiful and graceful hackles. Imitations can be kept simple. Woolly Buggers capture the action of the natural.** *Jim Schollmeyer*

The nymphs are burrowers. They are restricted to substrate types that are soft enough to allow tunneling yet firm enough not to collapse once excavation is complete. Populations are found in scattered locations across the entire continent. They are remarkably important wherever they are found.

Nymph

Hexagenia nymphs have three fringed tails. Their feathery and graceful gills ride up over the back of the abdominal segments. A pair of burrowing tusks at the head make them easy to recognize. They are so large that their imitations are tied on long-shank #6 and #8 hooks. Their color is a light tannish yellow.

Although it is a slight heresy, I recommend fishing a Brown Woolly Bugger for these large nymphs. It's a dressing that many of us carry because it looks like a lot of things, and it takes fish well in lots of situations. The movement of the marabou catches the swimming motion of the *Hexagenia* nymphs perfectly.

Brown Woolly Bugger

Hook: 3X long #6 to #8

Thread: Brown

Weight: 8 to 12 turns lead wire

Tail: Brown marabou

Hackle: Brown, palmered over body

Body: Brown chenille

Hexagenia have only one hatch per year. The nymphs live in muddy bottoms and survive down to the limits of light, feeding on detrital decay as long as they can get sufficient oxygen. They emerge in late spring or early summer, depending on temperatures and elevation. Actual emergence occurs just at dusk or after dark, and the nymph dressing is most important when naturals are swimming toward the surface to hatch. Because they are fast swimmers, undulating with the up-and-down movement of a leech, the imitation should be fished with a fast stripping retrieve.

Dun and Spinner

Both of the adult stages of *Hexagenia* can be important. Because the duns emerge at dusk or just after, and the spinners of a day or two before return to deposit their eggs shortly after that, the two can realistically be lumped together. Trout don't get the best look at either in the lack of light.

Duns have two tails, are veritable giants among mayflies, and are bright to faded yellow, depending on how soon you collect one after it emerges. Spinners are the same size, over an inch long in the body alone and with wings that stand up like barn doors. But they are glassy and clear rather than bright yellow.

Hexagenia **are the largest of mayfly duns, over an inch long and bright yellow when they first hatch. Their imitations must be large, like Polly Rosborough's Big Yellow May.** *Jim Schollmeyer*

Imitations should capture the size and silhouette of the natural first and its color secondarily because the light will be low when you fish them. Polly Rosborough's Big Yellow May, in either the dun or spinner version, works well. I'll give the spinner here and refer you to his book *Fuzzy Nymphs* for the dun dressing. But bear in mind that such odd patterns as a big Bucktail Caddis or Grizzly Wulff often do the same sort of devastation during a hatch.

Big Yellow May Spinner

Hook: 3X long #8

Thread: Tan

Tails: Yellow and ginger hackle fibers, mixed

Body: Yellow synthetic yarn

Wings: Dyed yellow deer hair, semispent

Hackle: Yellow and ginger, mixed

Hexagenia tend to hatch in May, June, and early July. Time of day is just at dark, slightly earlier on cloudy days. They emerge above any sort of bottom that will hold the nymphs, wherever the mud is right for their burrows, out to water fifteen or twenty feet deep.

When these duns come off, or the spinners return, at first you'll think you're seeing birds. Trout don't make the same mistake. They take them greedily, almost angrily. Set your imitation out on the water, let it sit a bit, then coax the fish by twitching it or even skating it if nothing happens. When a trout takes this large fly, you won't have any trouble telling about it.

CAENIS

In contrast to the giant *Hexagenia*, there are some tiny mayflies that you'll encounter on lakes from time to time. The extent of my personal experience with them doesn't qualify me to do much more than point out some possible solutions to them.

The one time I ran into minute *Caenis* mayflies on a lake – at dusk – the hatch wasn't heavy, trout failed to key in on them, and I kept fishing with what I had on since it continued to work. But then the little mayflies began lighting on my nylon wind jacket, and I stopped fishing altogether just to watch them. They were about a #20 or #22 and pure white. I was wading deep at the time, and they viewed me as the only solid object around. Dozens of duns landed on my sleeves until they were speckled white.

Then each one got a grip on me, split its dun skin, slowly molted into the spinner stage before my eyes, rested a moment,

**Tiny dressings like the Polywing Spinner work well when minute
mayflies are hatching and landing on the water.** *Jim Schollmeyer*

then flew away to mate in the air, lay its eggs, and die. It was one
of the most beautiful sights I've ever seen while fly-fishing; I can
tell you that *Caenis* are important if you are ever lucky enough to
see them happen, even if you never catch a fish over one.

To catch a fish over one, try simple Polywing Spinner dressings. They work as well for *Tricorythodes*, which are the same size
and shape, although they vary slightly in color. They also hatch on
lakes at scattered locations and times, and can be important if you
bump against them when trout feed selectively on them.

If you don't have some of these dressings handy when you run
into a hatch of minute mayflies, try trimming the bottom hackle
fibers from the nearest pattern you have, no matter its color. It's
always most important to capture the size and form of the natural
first and its color last.

Polywing Spinner

Hook: Standard dry fly, #20 to #24

Thread: White 8/0

Tails: Split white guard hairs or Micro Fibettes

Body: White fur or synthetic

Wings: White or light dun polypropylene yarn,
spent

16

Caddisflies

I have found caddisflies in stillwaters to be charmingly elusive. Caddis larvae in lakes and ponds are all cased, and although they're not all cryptic, they do live down among the weeds or directly on the bottom and do not often show up in trout stomach samples. The pupae are a brief transitional stage, bolting out of the case and to the top, or migrating to shore, in a way that you seldom see them. Rarely do the adults come off in such numbers and such ways that they constitute a concentrated hatch and cause selective feeding.

However, there are situations in which caddis become important. There is no doubt that trout eat lots more of them than ever gets noticed by anglers.

Caddis come in so many species, lumped into so many large families and genera, that addressing them by Latin name is an adventure in frustration. It's best to discuss and to understand them by their stages: larva, pupa, and adult.

Stillwater caddis la.vae often miscalculate their densities and wind up floating to the top when they'd rather sink to the bottom. Trout come along and pluck them, or imitations that look like them, such as this LaFontaine Cased Caddis. *Jim Schollmeyer*

LARVAE

Some caddis larvae live along wave-swept shorelines and build their cases of hard sand and pebbles for ballast against all the agitation. But most species live on the silty bottom, or in beds of vegetation, and build their cases of the same soft material on which they live. They are easily digested, case and all. That's the way trout eat them.

Recognizing caddis larvae is relatively easy, based on their transportable cases. No other stillwater forms possess them. All caddis larvae have six legs that protrude from the front of the case for locomotion, but only when the insect is not disturbed. They turn like turtles when bothered, withdrawing legs and heads into their cases. To confirm identification, prod or pluck a specimen from its case and look for its twin anal hooks. Evolution has replaced its tails with these. They serve to hold the larva in its case, which was why you had so much trouble extracting it.

Caddis larvae vary in size over a wide range, from #6 to #16 — the most common and most important being #10, #12, and #14. The body color is often white or cream to tan. But the color of the case is more significant, since that is what a trout will see and key on. The case will be the same color as the predominant vegetation: olive to tan.

I rarely use exact imitations of caddis larvae, finding instead that Woolly Worms, or Woolly Buggers with their tails pinched off, work well enough. But Gary LaFontaine's Cased Caddis is a miracle of imitation, and you should be familiar with it in case you encounter a situation where a lesser approximation of the natural fails to trigger responses from trout.

Cased Caddis

Hook: Standard length, #6 to #14 (bend front one-fourth up with pliers)

Thread: Brown or olive

Case: 2 to 4 soft feathers, palmered and clipped

Neck: White chenille

Legs: Brown or black hackle fibers

You can vary the feathers chosen to match the colors of whatever naturals you encounter. A combination of brown and olive saddle hackles or partridge feathers averages out to look like most common caddis larvae. You can weight the fly to fish it on the bottom. I fish it so often near the surface, and so slowly, that I prefer to leave it unweighted in order to keep from getting it hung up. If I want to get it down, I can do it with a sinking line.

This larval pattern is effective through spring and into summer — as long as caddis are still around. After midsummer most hatches have happened. There aren't so many cased caddis larvae still crawling around out there to attract the attention of trout.

The time of day to use caddis larval imitations is rather non-specific. These clumsy characters bumble about in weed beds all day long. Trout will pick them off whenever they see them. Try them whenever you perceive some sort of hint that they might work. The first clue is cased caddis visible on the bottom or crawling around in weed beds or on reed stems. The second clue is undigested vegetation in any stomach samples you might take. These are the remains of cased caddis.

Larval behavior is simple: They crawl slowly, or in the rare case of the Leptoceridae, swim feebly. The crawling types depend on a neutral buoyancy to maintain their position in the water column if they lose their grip on a reed stem or weed bed. During periods of changing barometric pressure I've seen them get their densities screwed up, causing them to float slowly to the top when they lose their grip on vegetation. This is usually fatal; trout come along and gulp them like grapes. That's why I leave my caddis larval patterns unweighted: I can fish them right on top.

Presentation, whether on the bottom, near the top, or anywhere in between, should be with a slow hand-twist retrieve. That's the speed at which cased caddis move. Use your line sink rate and leader length to achieve the depth you want. But remember that your retrieve will be so slow that the line will continue to tug the fly down beyond where you want it if you choose a line that sinks too fast. I've found the dry line and long leader perfect for most shallow situations, the wet-tip and a 7- to 8-foot leader best when I want to dangle the fly down toward submerged weed beds.

PUPAE

Caddis pupae are the most elusive of the three stages. In truth, I've seldom seen one in the wild—in stillwaters—except in stomach samples. The few I've seen on the loose were loners, swimming agilely near the surface out in open water, heading toward shore or some other destination known only to them.

I've seen schools of trout cruising in clear water at times when adult caddis were up top, and I have seen an individual fish suddenly dart out of the school to gun something down. I know the

Caddis pupae are a brief transitional stage, hard to collect . . . but imitations such as this LaFontaine Sparkle Pupa will take trout well.
Jim Schollmeyer

death of a caddis pupa happened there. But I can't prove it short of stomach samples, which I was reluctant to take.

Caddis pupae have soft and portly bodies, wing cases that slant back along their sides, and long antennae that trail over their backs. Their legs are fringed with hairs that turn them into effective paddles. Some of the naturals can swim very fast, which is another reason they are so elusive.

Like the larvae, stillwater caddis pupae range in size from #6 to #16. Some of the best imitations are simple soft hackles, but again Gary LaFontaine has captured some magic in his brilliant book *Caddisflies*, and his Sparkle Pupa takes more fish for me now when I suspect trout are feeding on caddis pupae.

Sparkle Pupa

Hook: Standard dry fly, #8 to #16

Thread: Olive or tan

Weight: 6 to 10 turns lead wire

Underbody: Olive or tan Sparkle Yarn

Overbody: Olive or tan Sparkle Yarn

Hackle: Ginger or brown

Head: Hare's mask fur, Hareline #4

The two colors given here are the most common, but they're just a start. Caddis pupae come in many colors. Use these two to begin with, and add others as you collect other colors over the years and find need for them. LaFontaine lists fifteen variations, and the pages of his book are an excellent reference.

The season of importance for caddis pupae tends toward spring and early summer, when most caddis hatches happen. They taper off in fall, although there are so many species that a few of them are sure to violate any attempts at pinning them down. It's always wise to have a few caddis pupal patterns handy.

Time of day is just as elusive as the naturals themselves. I suspect that the majority of them hatch at night. But I've seen specimens during all the daylight hours, most often at dawn and again at dusk.

Caddis habitat is associated with vegetation. But many pupal caddis migrate toward shore before emerging, so all of the water between the limits of vegetation growth and the shore itself becomes potential caddis water. Most often, think in terms of weed beds or shallows and you'll have it right.

The naturals swim right along, usually without many pauses to rest. Their trajectory is usually almost straight upward for an emergence at the surface. But those that migrate before emergence swim laterally through the water, often right on top. Your presentations should be based on one or the other of these two behaviors.

In the first instance use a weighted fly to get the fly down at the end of a long leader and a floating line. When it's down, lift the rod and retrieve at the same time to raise the fly from the bottom toward the surface in an unbroken motion, imitating a caddis pupa bolting for the top. For those that swim toward shore, simply cast out and let the fly sink to the depth you want, either near the top or bottom, not often in the middepths. Then use a modest to fast stripping retrieve to scoot the fly right along.

Trout will often wallop it.

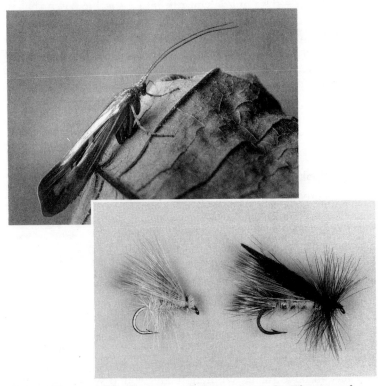

Many stillwater caddis forms are called "traveling sedges" because of their habit of motoring around on the water. The best imitations for them are patterns that can be skated on the surface, such as the Elk Hair Caddis and Vincent Sedge. *Jim Schollmeyer*

ADULTS

The most important stillwater caddis adults are known as traveling sedges because of their habit of motoring around on top like boats with abandoned tillers. But there are many caddis species that emerge on the surface and sit quiescent until they are able to take wing, or until a trout takes them. Patterns for the two types of behavior are slightly different. One needs to look right when it moves, the other when it's sitting still.

Caddis adults are recognized by their tentlike wings, absence of tails, and long antennae. They range from giant #6 specimens down to many as small as #16. Those that are most important run the midrange from #10 to #14, and most of your imitations should be tied in those sizes unless you run into a specific hatch that is either smaller or larger.

Although there are many imitation styles that work, I've found the Elk Hair Caddis excellent because you can fish it with its hackles intact and skitter it across the water, or trim its hackles on the bottom and show the trout an accurate silhouette of the sitting naturals.

Elk Hair Caddis

Hook: Standard dry fly, #8 to #16

Thread: Tan

Rib: Fine gold wire

Body: Tan fur or synthetic

Hackle: Ginger, palmered over body, held down with rib

Wing: Tan elk hair

The dressing as listed is effective most often, but a couple of variations are worth carrying. The first has a peacock herl body and grizzly hackle tucked under a brown deerhair wing. The second has an olive fur or synthetic body wound with a blue dun hackle beneath a natural gray deerhair wing. With these three you have lots of the natural color spectrum covered.

Another caddis adult dressing is designed specifically to imitate the action of a traveling sedge. It was designed for the Kamloops area of British Columbia, known for its sedge hatches and heavy trout.

Vincent Sedge

Hook: 1X or 2X long #10 to #12

Thread: Black

Tail: Deer body hair, short

Rib: Narrow green floss

Body: Light olive green seal fur or wool

Underwing: Deer body hair

Overwing: Mottled turkey primary, lacquered

Hackle: Brown, tied thick

This dressing condensed my memories from a week-long trip to a British Columbia lake into a single instant. Rick Hafele eased the canoe along a rocky shoreline while I cast a Vincent Sedge against the rocks, let it sit a moment, then skittered it out a few feet. The fly worked perfectly, leaving a V-wake behind, refusing to sink.

As we approached a large boulder Rick said, "A good one rose there." I didn't see the rise, but cast to the spot, let the fly rest, then skated it a foot. A nose rose out, the fly disappeared in a solid swirl, and I set the hook into a 2-pound Kamloops rainbow that dashed into the air to see what had happened to it. A few minutes later it came thrashing into the net.

It was far from the biggest fish on the trip; it didn't even put up the boldest fight. But it made the nicest rise. When I lean back and close my eyes and recall the trip, that nose arising and engulfing the fly is the vision that comes instantly to my mind.

17

Midges

The midge is an insect belonging to the insect family Chironomidae. The more common use of the word means "any small fly." True midges are members of the two-winged order Diptera. They are related to the houseflies that buzz around and bother you. They're also related to mosquitoes, which do more than buzz around and bother you. Midges aren't much of a bother, except that they inspire rises of trout that can be damningly hard to solve.

Most but not all midges are small, some so tiny that they can't be imitated with any existing hooks. But some are so large they must be imitated with #8 flies tied on long-shank hooks.

Midges come in about one thousand different species. Like caddis, they are best understood by looking at their progressive stages.

LARVAE

I don't attach much importance to midge larvae, although trout do. They are taken in great numbers by fish. They typically burrow around in dense vegetation, or even in the bottom silts if enough oxygen exists down there. They're not taken in situations where trout become selective to them, at least in my experience. Whenever I find trout feeding on or near the bottom, I also find midge larvae in stomach samples. But they are mixed with other inhabitants of the same zone, expressing the trout's interest in anything that moves and looks reasonable to eat.

When I choose to fish that zone, I prefer to do it with larger flies imitating beasts that can be copied more closely and presented more realistically. Midge larvae swim with a whiplike coiling and uncoiling of the body that is not only difficult to duplicate but essentially directionless. They don't have either eyes or rudders. They whip along at random. It's hard to make a fly do the same thing.

Dragonflies, damselflies, and leeches all manage most of their movement in the forward direction, which makes it easier to present something plausible before the eyes of a trout. Since that trout is not likely to be selective, anyway, it makes life a lot easier if you imitate something besides midge larvae.

PUPAE

The importance of the midge to the trout fisherman lies in this pivotal stage between larva and adult. Pupation takes place in a crude shelter built by the larva and attached to vegetation or burrowed into the bottom. When pupation is complete, the insect drifts free and rises to the surface with a combination of positive buoyancy and a feeble swimming motion. But it's not a fast transition like that of the caddis. Many helpless midge pupae are taken by trout throughout the entire water column, from bottom to top.

Midge pupae can be recognized by the short swimming paddles on the last abdominal segment, the numerous fine respiratory filaments in the thoracic region, and the closely coupled head and thorax, giving the insect a humpbacked or bunched appearance at the head end. They range from #8 down to #26. Their colors run almost the full range of the spectrum. Most common are light cream, tan, brown, green, black, and red. If I had time to tie only two dressings, which unfortunately is usually the case, they would be green and black, in #12 to #18.

Midge pupae bump into the surface film and are forced to hang there until they can break through. Imitations such as the TDC (left) and Buzzer Pupa should be fished on a greased leader, very near the surface. *Jim Schollmeyer*

The best imitations capture the swimmer paddles and respiratory filaments at the ends, the slender body between, and the bunched and somewhat darker thorax and head. The most successful single imitation I've used is Richard Thompson's TDC.

Black is a common color in the midge family. It is not uncommon to take trout with the black TDC even when the hatching midges are another color. I've mentioned it before: If I'm fishing a battery of two flies in order to explore a stillwater, the lead fly will

TDC

Hook: 1X or 2X long #10 to #16

Thread: Black

Rib: Narrow silver tinsel

Body: Black wool yarn

Thorax: Black chenille

Collar: White ostrich herl

almost always be a #12 or #14 TDC. It has taken a lot of trout for me, in selective and nonselective situations.

But you need a pattern style to fall back on so you can create imitations in the correct size and color when you encounter a midge hatch and feeding trout that are snooty about what they believe matches the hatch. Since there are more than one thousand species, you will run into these situations if you fish lakes more than once or twice a year.

One of the most attractive and effective styles I've seen is found in Taff Price's fine British book, *Fly Patterns, an International Guide*. It's called the Buzzer Pupa.

Buzzer Pupa

Hook: Standard dry fly #10 to #16

Thread: Black

Tail: Tuft of white floss

Body: Black floss

Rib: Silver wire

Thorax: Bronze peacock herl

Breathing filaments: White floss

This is the base pattern. You can work all sorts of color variations on it and would be wise to do so. I've used it successfully in black, tan, and green.

Another dressing that I've found useful when the smallest midges hatch doesn't necessarily have a name, nor does it need one. It is simply a few turns of dubbing wound on a hook shank. It's a fly that I use a lot when nymphing the bottom in spring creeks and tailwaters. It has worked well for me when trout feed on a specific color of midge pupa in a stillwater, and I don't have anything near it in my fly boxes. It's easy to tie this generic fly in a range of colors and sizes. Its usefulness is not restricted to midge situations.

The season of midge importance is not restricted, either. They hatch all year around, whenever the weather is not so blustery that the adults can't escape into the air and fly away. They'll come out on cold winter days if the air is relatively calm, usually in the warmest part of the day. They'll hatch on midsummer days so hot the sun scorches you, although usually in the cool of morning or evening. Spring hatches are often heavy. Fall hatches are some of the best. Midges are out there happening all year around. They take up the slack when something larger, and therefore easier to imitate, is not around absorbing the trout's attention.

Larval habitat extends into the profundal zone. As a consequence, midge pupal emergences take place out in the pelagial zone far from the shoreline. In fact, the first thing to suspect when you see trout rising in midwater, where you're always surprised to see them, is midge pupae. You'll usually be right.

Two bits of midge pupa behavior suggest two ways to fish their imitations. In the first the pupae leave their larval cases and float slowly up through the water column toward the surface. Trout intercept them on the entire trip, and you have to get your fly down where it happens. To do this, the fly must be weighted. But in order to keep its posture upward, it's best to fish it on a floating line and very long leader, sometimes as long as 20 or even 25 feet. You should know by now that you have to straighten your leader diligently when it's this long, or you'll never see the darting line tip that registers a take.

The fly, when fished this way, should be allowed to simply idle along, or at most it should be retrieved with a hand-twist retrieve that tugs it forward and toward the surface at the same time.

The second bit of behavior happens when the ascending pupa bumps against the restrictions of the surface film. A small, slowly moving insect doesn't have much force to put against this wall, and it takes a long time for it to break through. This is most true on calm days, when the tension is greatest, least true on rough days, when the tension is broken up and the insect can get through it easily.

To duplicate this second set of problems it's best to fish an unweighted midge pupa. Dress your leader with floatant down to about six to twelve inches from the fly. That causes it to suspend just beneath the surface and to catch the eye of trout plucking naturals from the surface film.

Because these two ways of fishing midge pupae call for weighted and unweighted versions of the same fly, it's best to work out a few favorite dressings and tie them both ways. Be sure to devise some system for keeping them apart – use different colors of thread, or separate fly boxes, so you know which one you're fishing when the situation arises. I'm not very good at keeping my weighted and unweighted flies separate because of the confusion in my fly boxes. It costs me frustration and fish.

ADULTS

Midge adults, like their larvae, are not of great importance to the fisherman. But they can't be dismissed so lightly. There is a common hitch in their progress from pupa to adult that gives some individuals magnified importance. These are the stillborns. They get stuck in the pupal shuck and are unable to struggle free from the surface film. When enough individuals develop these troubles, trout begin to feed selectively on them. You have to match them or go without action.

It's not easy to tell when this kind of behavior is going on. Sometimes you'll actually see midges stuck in the surface, struggling feebly. But more often you'll simply see rises, not be able to see what the trout are taking, and not be able to catch the trout no matter what you toss at them. It's a situation that is solved more often by hunch than by precise observation.

It boils down to this: When nothing else works, try matching midges in the surface film. Even that might fail. I just spent three days camped on a small lake, had brief and mysterious rises each morning, but could never solve them before the trout quit rising.

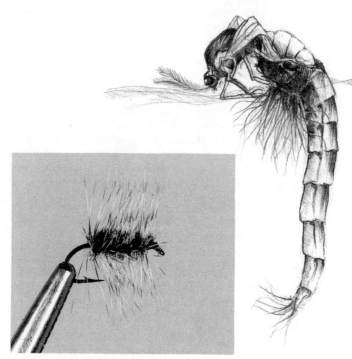

When stillborn midges become available in great numbers, trout key on them, and the best imitation becomes a Griffith's Gnat fished awash in the film. *Jim Schollmeyer*

The single fish I caught, on a streamer, was stuffed with tiny zooplankton, which didn't help solve the mystery.

It will surprise you how often a Griffith's Gnat, fished in the film, will take trout in such situations.

Griffith's Gnat

Hook: Standard dry fly, #16 to #22

Thread: Black

Body: Peacock herl

Hackle: Grizzly, palmered

That's all there is to it. It's one of the easiest flies to tie as long as you use quality hackle. It's one of the most effective to fish as long as you use fine tippets. Just cast it out and let it sit. If it doesn't draw trout, give it a nudge, enough to send out a tiny ripple but not enough to draw the fly under.

If that doesn't do it, and pupal patterns have failed, then trout are probably feeding on something besides midges.

18

Dragonflies and Damselflies

Dragonflies and damselflies are the aerial gunners of the insect world. They are agile in flight. They form a catching basket with their legs, then cruise a territory that is sometimes far from the water of their origins, capturing smaller insects, often devouring them in the air. Most of their prey is small – bless them for killing millions of mosquitoes. But I have also seen a dragonfly become the sudden ending of a big fall caddis and a damselfly drag a large moth down to death.

Adults of both groups return to water to lay eggs for the next generation and are taken by trout at times. The nymphs of both are strictly aquatic and are the most important stage to the fly fisherman.

DRAGONFLIES

Dragonflies are swift and dodging in flight and pugnacious in nature. They remind me of the light observation helicopters – Loaches – that flew low over Vietnam with their miniguns blazing angrily. Dragonflies buzz briskly in and out of trouble, hover to examine minutely anything that looks out of place, and dive to attack something that moves where it shouldn't.

The adults are fascinating to watch but not of great value to the angler. Many of us have seen trout try to take them. I've seen V-wakes well up under dragonflies flying low over the water and have witnessed a trout trying to capture one. Some people I've talked to have seen trout erupt and pluck dragonflies out of the air. But it doesn't happen often. I've also seen dragonflies land exhausted on the water, quiver there for an hour, and never get pestered by big trout that I knew were cruising in the area because I was busy catching them on Woolly Buggers.

Dragonflies have a two- or three-year life cycle. The nymphs, down underwater, are available to trout all year long. In contrast to the adults, they are very important to anglers.

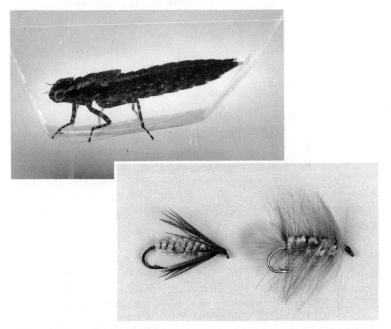

Dragonfly nymphs are big, blocky characters that have their own systems of jet propulsion. Imitations include the Carey Special (left) and a Woolly Bugger with its tails pinched short. *Jim Schollmeyer*

Dragonfly Nymphs

Dragonfly nymphs can be recognized by their hourglass shape, pinched in between the thorax and abdomen. They have large and observant eyes, three spiky tails at the end of the abdomen, and a hinged jaw beneath the head. This jaw is used at the end of a successful stalk; it unhinges abruptly, firing out to capture the nymph's prey.

Dragonfly nymphs are large, ranging from one to two inches long. Because they are rather portly, they offer a substantial mouthful to a trout. Imitations should be tied on hooks from #4, when the largest mature specimens are still around in early summer, down to #12 to imitate the second-year class after the larger nymphs have hatched and are busy flying about.

Colors copy the predominant vegetation in a lake or pond or the bottom color. They range from green to tan. The most common color I have collected over a wide geographic range is a mix of green and brown.

Carey Special

Hook: 3X long #6 to #12

Thread: Olive 6/0

Body: Olive chenille

Hackle: Pheasant rump

The Carey Special is tied most often as a specific for dragonfly nymphs. An Olive Woolly Worm works well, too. I have recently taken to fishing an Olive Woolly Bugger tied with brown hen hackle in #8 or #10 with about half of its marabou tail pinched off just before I cast it. This fly captures the approximate size and mixed colors of the natural. It also looks like a lot of other things. I don't know when the trout take it for a dragonfly nymph or when they mistake it for something else. But I do know that they take it often.

Of course, you can tie the tail short if you'd like, or pinch it to shape at the time of tying. But why limit your options? Tie the fly as a normal Woolly Bugger, then pinch its tails off at the time you

Pinched Woolly Bugger

Hook: 3X long #6 to #12
Thread: Olive
Weight: 10 to 15 turns lead wire
Tail: Olive marabou
Body: Olive chenille
Hackle: Brown hen

decide to fish it as a dragonfly nymph. There are lots of other things this fly can do if you leave its tails intact.

Dragonfly nymphs build up in importance through the spring and into early summer. Emergence takes place throughout that period and tapers off as the water gets warm and starts to stratify. The nymphs must migrate to shore, where they crawl out, lock themselves on a plant stem or shoreline rock, split along the back, and allow the slow exudation of the adult.

Emergence is a dangerous time for the dragonfly because it cannot move to escape predation while it escapes its own shuck. Most migrations toward shore take place in the evening, with emergence happening at dusk or even after, when birds have gone to bed. The most important time to fish their imitations is in the early part of the season, in the late part of the day.

But they're out there and available to fish all day long. Don't restrict use of their imitations to specific moments. Trout are aware of the naturals at all times and are always eager to snap at one.

Prime habitat for dragonfly nymphs is a shallow weed bed. But they are also found in good numbers in woody debris along the shoreline. The silter or crawler variety makes its living by camouflaging itself right in the bottom silt, then waiting for some smaller creature to wander within range of the spring of its jaw. When these types move, they creep.

The more common and more agile dragonfly nymphs, called swimmers, have a unique adaptation that lets them jet through the water. Their gills are in their abdomens, and they deliver fresh water to the gills through the anal orifice. The bulbed abdomen becomes a large storage tank for water. When startled the nymph clamps down its tummy structures and a powerful stream of water shoots out behind it, jetting the insect forward a few inches. This can be repeated quickly, and the nymph darts through the water without any apparent effort.

The two types of movement of the silters and swimmers suggest two types of presentation. The first is to let your fly achieve the bottom. Once it gets there, creep it along with a hand-twist retrieve. You can use this only over bottoms free of snags, but it works alarmingly well there. It probably recalls to the trout certain crawling cased caddis, as well, and triggers pickups that get reported up the line as stern, determined tugs.

The second type of retrieve, based on the jetlike swimming of the more agile types, is a fast strip. But keep each pull with your line hand short and abrupt. The retrieve should be jerky because that's the way the natural swims. Give it some pauses, as if the nymph halts to catch its breath. It can't go long distances with its afterburners on.

DAMSELFLIES

Damsels are shrunk and stretched versions of dragonflies in both the nymphal and adult stages. They have much of the same equipment, including a hinged jaw in the nymphal stage, and many of the same manners, such as capturing and devouring insects in the air as adults. Like the larger dragons, they are most important in the underwater stage. Unlike dragonflies, the adults often get onto the water and are taken eagerly by trout when they do. Both stages are worth consideration here.

Damselfly Nymphs

Damselfly nymphs are between one and two inches long and very slender. They have beadlike eyes, a hinged lower jaw, and caudal gills that used to be tails. These are the key characteristics for recognition. You can't mistake damselfly nymphs for anything else. Their tails look like veined willow leaves and are designed to extract oxygen out of the water and transport it to the cells of the nymph.

Colors of the naturals, like the colors of most aquatic crea-

Damselfly nymphs are long and slender, with willow-leaf gills for tails. Their imitations should capture the movement of the tails with marabou, as done by Polly Rosborough's Green Damsel (left) and the modified Woolly Bugger. *Jim Schollmeyer*

tures, are those of the substrate on which they live. The most common variations I have collected are bright green and shades of olive mixed with brown.

Imitations range in size from #8 down to #12, tied on long-shank hooks to capture the elongated shape of the natural. The most common dressing—and one of the best—is Polly Rosborough's Green Damsel. It uses marabou to capture the shape as well as the movement of the damsel.

The pattern I use just as often to imitate damselfly nymphs is another conversion of an Olive Woolly Bugger, not far removed from the one I use to fish for dragonfly nymphs. I'll give its dressing here.

Green Damsel

Hook: 3X long #8 to #10

Thread: Olive

Tail: Light green marabou

Body: Green fur or yarn

Wing case: Green marabou

Legs: Teal flank dyed olive

Damsel Nymph

Hook: Standard length, 2X stout #10 to #12

Thread: Olive

Weight: 8 to 12 turns fine lead wire

Tail: Olive marabou

Body: Olive chenille

Hackle: Brown hen, 2 to 3 turns over front one-third of body, trimmed top and bottom

The long marabou tail on this fly represents both the body and the caudal gills of the natural. The sparse hackle represents the legs, and is soft hen so the fibers will collapse back against the sides of the fly during the retrieve, just as the legs of the natural are folded along its sides when it swims.

The season for damsels is approximately the same as that for dragonflies: spring and early summer. But they have a one-year life cycle and are not available in first- and second-year classes after the hatch dwindles down in midsummer. So their usefulness is restricted to the early part of the season. Preferred habitat is dense weed beds, although they are also found hunting in sparse forests of pondweed. Their sticklike bodies are camouflage as they hug the stems of plants. They are not often found hunting the bottom itself.

Although cryptic when among the weeds, hiding and stalking prey, damsels suddenly become swimmers when the urge to emerge strikes them. Like dragonflies, they must make the migration to shore, where they crawl out on exposed vegetation or shoreline structures before the adult escapes the nymphal skin. Most migrations take place in afternoon and evening, with the vulnerable hatch happening at dusk or after dark.

If the weed bed of their origins is far from shore and does not extend to the surface, damsels often must swim a quarter mile or more in open water. Trout are aware of this problem and take advantage of it with bold swirls. If the nymphs are near the top, which they often are, then it can appear to the casual observer that trout are taking something off the surface. Whenever you see fish feeding with bold boils in spring or early summer but can't see anything on the surface, suspect damsels and give the nymphs a try.

Their swimming motion is a side-to-side undulation. Although they are capable of bursts of speed, most of their progress is slow and laborious, interspersed with periods when they put on the brakes and rest. During these rests they slowly sink toward the bottom. There are, therefore, three parts to the movement of migrating damsels. You have to be aware of all three because trout might key in on one of them and ignore a nymph retrieved in a manner that copies one of the others.

First, damsels swim with that slow, undulating movement. That is why marabou is so good in their imitations: It captures the internal movements at a slow speed of retrieve. Second, damsels put on bursts of speed when they have to, and one can assume that they feel they have to when a trout looms into view. Third, a damsel must rest in its travels toward a distant shore.

Basing retrieves on the behavior of the naturals is simple when you know about all this. To mimic the slow swim, use a hand-twist retrieve and trust the movement of your marabou to entice the fish. To copy the sudden burst of speed, use a fast stripping retrieve and add some twitching with the rod tip to make the progress of the nymph sporadic, as if it's swimming in panic to escape something. Finally, to rest your nymph, simply stop the retrieve and let the fly sit and slowly sink.

In my own experience most takes come when the fly is at rest.

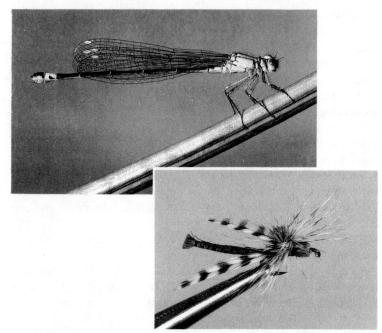

Adult damselflies take wing only when the sun is out and the wind is down. Imitations, such as John Shewey's Adult Damsel, should be fished along reed edges and the shoreline. *Jim Schollmeyer*

They are, of course, the most difficult takes to detect, which is why it is mandatory to fish damsels with a leader that has been carefully stretched and straightened.

The most logical way to fish damsels is to combine all three sorts of retrieve into one cast. Cast the fly out and let it sink, then hand-twist it in for a few feet. Give it a sudden shot of speed and agitated action, then let it rest. Then go through the cycle again.

If you find trout accepting one part of the retrieve and ignoring the others, then concentrate on the one and forget the others.

Damselfly Adults

Adult damsels can be recognized by their slender bodies, lack of tails, beadlike eyes on the sides of the head, and two pairs of clear wings. Because their size overlaps with some smaller dragonflies, there is often confusion between the two. Separating them is simple: Dragons hold their wings out to the sides when at rest, and damsels hold them extended over the back.

Most damsel adults are in the size range that would be tied on #10 and #12 long-shank hooks, although it's often wise to tie them on short-shank hooks and use an extended body of some sort. The most common color is blue, usually a very bright blue.

John Shewey's Adult Damsel

Hook: Standard dry fly, #10 or #12

Thread: Black

Body: Bright blue bucktail bound with working thread

Wing post: Butts of body hair

Hackle: Grizzly or blue dun, parachute, oversized

Wings: Grizzly or blue dun hackle tips (optional)

Damsel adults enjoy a long season: through the entire spring and summer as long as the weather stays warm. They have a habit of flying only when the sun shines. If the wind comes up, they retreat to vegetation. If a cloud passes over, they cease to fly. But wind often knocks them off their perches on reed stems and lily pads near the water. Whenever this happens, trout cruise the shoreline and feed on them anxiously, with strong takes.

It's always best to fish a dry fly on the sit at first. If that fails to interest trout, then give it a twitch, or even skate it along, making it mimic a damsel feathering over the water in search of a place to deposit its eggs.

19

Alderflies

Rick Hafele and I have a mild disagreement over alderflies. If you haven't met him, Rick is a professional aquatic entomologist, author of fly-fishing books, and talent in the videotape "Anatomy of a Trout Stream." He thinks alderflies are not important to the fly fisherman. I think they are. But I think they're about as important as the degree of our disagreement: only mildly.

I fish lots of alder-rimmed ponds. Naturally that's where you find lots of alderflies. Rick fishes waters that are more often lined with conifers or surrounded by sagebrush. They aren't very good habitat for the natural larvae. They have small to negligible populations of alderflies.

Alderfly larvae are fierce predators that hunt among silt and leaf-packs right along the bottom. Their populations are highest where the silt is most energetic: loaded with tiny prey organisms. That means midge larvae, because that is what alderfly larvae are most able to capture and consume.

So you begin to get the picture of an alderfly pond. It is hemmed in by trees that sprinkle leaves onto the water. Its bottom

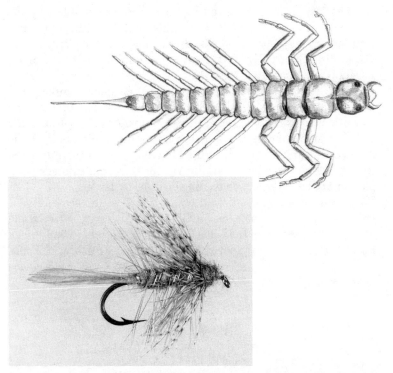

Alderfly larvae are cryptic, crawling around in the bottom leaf packs, but they're often taken by trout. Imitations such as the Alder Larva, fished just on the bottom, will fool the fish. *Jim Schollmeyer*

has the kind of composition that coaxes you to step into the edges where you slowly keep sinking, until you wonder if you'll stop before you've reached the tops of your waders. A black cloud of dirty water wells up around your legs, and the disturbance you've caused often releases a great benthic fart of organic decay.

Alderfly ponds are usually eutrophic. The water is often tannic and dark. The leaves on the bottom can sometimes be lifted out in a compact mass, then separated as if you were turning the pages of a book. On one page you find the prey. Turn a page or two and you expose the angry alderfly larva. Put your finger where the larva can reach it and it will try to pinch you with its mandibles, which are awesome.

The larvae are recognized by these fierce mandibles, by the lateral spines that are actually gill filaments, and by the single terminal process that could also be called a tail. They range from #10 to #14. Their color is light tan to brown, with a line of markings down the back.

Even I agree that the larvae are not of particular importance, although trout take them. Emergence takes place in the new warmth of late May through early July. Pupation takes place in the soil alongside the lake or pond. The larvae must migrate to shore, crawl out, and construct the pupal burrow. During the migration trout predation is substantial. But I've never seen a stomach sample that indicated selective feeding on alderfly larvae.

However, an appropriate dressing fished at this time of year will draw takes. I usually use a Gold-Ribbed Hare's Ear or some other generic dressing. But I like this one that I found in Taff Price's *Fly Patterns*. It was originated by the famous British angler and writer C. F. Walker. I am violating the rule that one should never write about a pattern he has never fished.

Alder Larva

Hook: Long shank #10 to #12

Thread: Brown or black

Tail: Honey cock hackle tip

Body: Mixed brown and ginger seal's fur or substitute

Rib: Oval gold tinsel

Hackle: Honey hen hackle palmered; head hackle brown partridge

Thorax: Hare's ear fur

This dressing, or a Gold-Ribbed Hare's Ear, should be fished right on the bottom with a slow hand-twist retrieve. It's best to leave the fly unweighted and use the appropriate sink rate line to get the fly down. The bottom is a bad place to put a fly in most typical alderfly habitat. I haven't seen a lake or pond with good

The alderfly adult is a caddisfly look-alike, but it has a dense body, and sinks when it lands on the water. Imitations that work best for it are wet flies, such as the old Alder. *Jim Schollmeyer*

populations of them that wasn't so snaggy you could execute more than two or three casts and retrieves before losing a fly. Perhaps that's why I don't imitate the larvae specifically, preferring to fish the adult dressing, which I do consider important.

Alderfly adults look almost exactly like big black caddisflies. They have a blocky, prehistoric appearance. The other features that distinguish them from caddis are a wide segment behind the head, rather than the wasp-waisted neck of the caddis, and a lack of fine hairs on the wings, which are parchmentlike rather than feathery.

At first glance it would seem that you could imitate alders with your favorite caddis dressing tied black. But it doesn't work that way. Alderflies have a terrific knack for bad flight, and they land on the water with a smack. They also have a high specific density. When they land on the water, they might rest there a moment, but most of the time they simply sink. And that's the way trout see them.

The best dressing for the adult alderfly is therefore a wet fly: the venerable Alder.

Alder

Hook: Standard wet fly, #10 to #12

Thread: Black

Rib: Narrow gold tinsel (optional)

Body: Peacock herl

Hackle: Black hen

Wings: Dark brown turkey tail-feather sections

I've been working a variation on this pattern lately, although I haven't found that it works any better than the standard tie. It's easier to tie, though, and works at least as well. Instead of the turkey wing, which is difficult to find anymore, I substitute a thick clump of the same black hen used for the hackle. It is more mobile in the water than turkey quill, and it makes me feel like the fly entices the fish with its movement. It might be true.

Alderflies are clumsy fliers, and it's easy to see when a few are in the air. They fly during the heat of a hot day, and their presence is always sporadic. But trout are aware of them, and you'll see occasional swirls that mark the end of one of them. Even if the swirl marks the end of something else, the fish will usually come to a wet Alder presented correctly.

The presentation should be at the end of a floating line and standard dry-fly leader. You'll want to fish the fly just inches deep. The most promising way to fish it is by casting it right into the departing rings of a rise. Then draw in enough line to remove slack and let the fly sit. What it does is slowly sink, just like the natural does after it falls through the surface film. You've got to be very alert. If the take comes while the fly is still near the top, you'll see the swirl. But if it comes after the fly has plunged a bit, you'll just see the leader or line tip twitch. Set the hook.

My most common mistake when fishing the wet Alder is to begin the retrieve too soon and too fast. A hand-twist is all right after the fly has been in the water awhile. But a stripping retrieve does not mimic the behavior of the natural at all.

I use a stripping retrieve as a way of getting the fly back in preparation for the cast to the next rise. But it's actually a wasted part of the cast most of the time. Some small trout come to it. Even some smart trout pluck at it. But the retrieved Alder wet has to be moving very slowly to fool the kind of fish you'd like to brag about.

20

Water Boatmen and Back Swimmers

Because they have life cycles and contrary habits that put them in contrast to more typical aquatic insects, water boatmen and back swimmers have certain moments of stillwater importance. Although they are not great moments, it is still wise to know about them so you can take advantage of them when they happen.

WATER BOATMEN

Water boatmen have a one-year life cycle. They exit from the egg in spring, then grow all through summer and fall when other aquatic insects are busy emerging, laying their eggs, and dying. As a result, water boatmen reach maturity in late fall when other insects are in their immature stages. They are largest and most available to trout when other insects are smallest and least available. Trout often turn their attention to the more mature food form.

Water boatmen have a beetlelike carapace formed of their forewings, which are held forward and out of the way when the

Water boatmen have long oarlike legs that propel them around like little rowboats. Their imitations, like this Water Boatman, should be fished shallow with twitching retrieves. *Jim Schollmeyer*

insect takes wing for spring egg-laying flights. They have sucking mouthparts, with which they probe into the cells of aquatic plant stems to pry out nutritive juices. Their front legs are scoop-shaped, used for winnowing through the periphyton, shoveling up and eating edible bits of it. If a juicy midge larva gets scooped up with the ooze, they eat it. But most of their diet consists of vegetable matter.

The hind legs of water boatmen are adapted for swimming. They make powerful oars, stroking the insect along. Water boatmen swim in what would be considered a normal fashion, with their backs toward the surface, which doesn't seem to make much difference until we consider their close relatives the back swimmers, whose manner of swimming you should be able to guess by now.

Water boatmen vary from #16 up to #12. Their color is always in sync with the vegetation on which they live. Most are mottled colors of olive and tannish brown. A successful imitation captures the salient features: the carapace back and oarlike legs.

Water Boatman

Hook: 1X long #12 to #16

Thread: Olive or tan

Weight: 4 to 8 turns fine lead wire

Shellback: Natural or green-dyed turkey quill

Body: Green or tan chenille

Oar legs: Single pheasant-tail fibers to each side

In #16 I usually use a ball of dubbing wrapped over a half dozen turns of thin lead wire. This rough dressing is close enough to the natural and easy enough to tie. In larger sizes I use the Water Boatman dressing as listed.

Water boatmen dash to the surface and capture a bubble of air under the carapace. After it submerges, the insect extracts the oxygen it needs from the bubble. Because they must refresh the bubble from time to time, water boatmen are restricted to the top two to four feet of the water column. Because the bubble is buoyant, they need to hold on to vegetation to keep themselves down. Their habitat is restricted to weed beds or submerged plant stems that are no more than about two to four feet deep. They are creatures of the shoreline and shallows, and that's where you should fish their imitations.

Water boatmen swim quite briskly, with sweeps of the legs that propel them in little darts. I have found the best presentation to visible and cruising fish is a straightforward cast that places the fly in the path of the fish. Let it sink slowly, depending on the slight weight to help it along, and hope it catches the eye of the fish and entices it. If this does not happen, begin a stripping retrieve while vibrating the rod tip, causing the fly to dart along like the natural.

When fishing the fly over fish that you suspect are down there but cannot see, use the stripping retrieve with a throbbing rod tip.

A floating line and long leader work perfectly at the depths you will want to fish. But do give the fly a few moments to sink before beginning the retrieve.

BACK SWIMMERS

Back swimmers are closely related to water boatmen and also have a one-year life cycle that increases their importance in fall. But they have another bit of behavior that is unique in the insect world and that makes them important when other insects are not. They are the only insect predator to follow pelagic midge hatches out into open water, feeding on pupae that slowly ascend to the surface from the profundal depths. But back swimmers are restricted to the surface, where they must get their bubble of air for oxygen. So they hang from the rafters of the surface, waiting for midges to come to them.

Sometimes what arrives is a trout, not a midge.

The results are remarkably different when that happens. The back swimmer dives and swims furiously away with strokes of its oar legs. I don't know how often they make their escape, but I know it's not always because I've seen bold boils out in open water and have later caught trout that contained back swimmers bulging in their diets.

Whenever I see vigorous rises in open water, the kind of boils that I know a trout would make when taking something large that can escape, not something tiny that can't, then I suspect they are feeding on back swimmers, not midges.

Back swimmers have a beetlelike carapace similar to water boatmen. They also have sucking mouthparts, although theirs are designed to penetrate the skins of prey rather than the walls of plant cells. The front legs of the back swimmer end in raptorial claws rather than scoops. Their oar legs are very similar to those of water boatmen, but back swimmers swim upside down.

Back-swimmer imitations should be tied on #10 and #12 hooks, on the average a size or so larger than water boatmen. Many specimens are mottled olive in color and are hard to distinguish from water boatmen except by their manner of swimming. The same imitations will fish as well for either insect.

The majority of back swimmers that I've collected or found in

The back swimmer swims briskly and upside down. The Prince Nymph might be such an effective imitation because the white wings represent the sheen of the natural's bubble of air. *Jim Schollmeyer*

stomach samples fall into the category that Ernest Schwiebert, in his beautiful book *Nymphs*, gave the poetic name Pale Moon-Winged Backswimmers. It describes them perfectly: They are nearly pure white. No doubt it is camouflage from below. They blend in with the sky above.

Strangely, the best imitation I have found for these is the Prince Nymph, with white goose biots held over its back. These capture both the white of the natural and, I also suspect, the sheen of the bubble of air.

I discovered the effectiveness of this dressing once while fishing for brook trout and rainbows feeding on a hatch of midges far from the shoreline of a mountain lake. Most of the time the trout fed daintily, taking midges, but an occasional sudden boil spoke of something else.

I tried the Prince Nymph and took several fish. The two I kept for dinner contained hundreds of #32 or smaller midge pupae, too

Prince Nymph

Hook: 1X long #10 to #12

Thread: Black

Tails: 2 black goose biots

Rib: Fine silver tinsel

Body: Peacock herl

Hackle: Brown hen, sparse and short

Wing: White goose biots, tied to sides, length of body

small for me to imitate, although perhaps not too small for you. But each of the stomachs held two or three back swimmers, standing out large in the stew of midges. The trout seemed willing to mistake the Prince Nymph for a back swimmer, which was their undoing.

Most of the time back swimmers are associated with shallow vegetation, and their imitations should be fished there. But I fish them most often specifically as imitations when trout feed away from shore, because I know they are more likely to be keyed to them in that situation.

The naturals swim with long, bold strokes, pausing to rest occasionally. Fish the imitations with a stripping retrieve, near the surface on a floating line, and intersperse the fast retrieve with intermittent pauses.

21

Scuds and Other Crustaceans

Scuds are likely in a tie with leeches as the most important non-insect food form for trout in stillwaters. Scuds pose a single problem: They don't hatch, as insects do. They mate underwater instead, and all year long, so that it's difficult to gauge their presence and importance in a particular water without doing some careful snooping.

You have to do some collecting, or else take some stomach samples, before you know scuds are around. But they're well worth the effort. Their perpetually aquatic life-style means they're always available to trout.

Other crustaceans include cress bugs, also called water sow-bugs, and crayfish. Both are peripheral in importance, taking distant second seats to scuds.

SCUDS

Recognition of scuds is easy. They have curved chitinous backs, no clear distinction between the abdomen and thorax regions, and an

Natural scuds curl up into a half circle when taken from the water, but they're straight as sticks when they swim. Their imitations, such as this Olive Scud, should capture the straight posture, not the curve.
Jim Schollmeyer

excess of legs along the entire underbody, most of which are actually swimmer paddles.

Scuds vary in size from minute, when they are immature, to some that are large enough to imitate with flies tied on #10 and #12 hooks. Their color is a camouflage against the vegetation or bottom type on which they live. That means they are most often green, sometimes tan or gray. But they change color quickly when pickled in alcohol or when eaten by a trout. If you observe scuds as collected specimens, note their colors before they change. Later they might be pink, bright orange, or faded white. But that's not what trout see and eat.

I've had great success fishing Gold-Ribbed Hare's Ears and Zug Bugs as imitations of scuds. But more exact patterns serve better when trout become selective to them, which they do at odd times throughout the season.

Olive Scud

Hook: 1X long #10 to #14

Thread: Olive

Weight: 8 to 12 turns fine lead wire (optional)

Tail: Olive hackle fibers

Shellback: Clear plastic

Rib: Olive thread

Body: Olive-gray seal mixed with olive rabbit fur

Legs: Olive hackle

Antennae: Wood duck flank fibers

This is the standard dressing for the scud. It can be varied in color to match others that you collect in your own waters. I confess that most of the time when I tie scud patterns for my own fishing, I omit the tails and antennae as unnecessary refinements. It's a laziness that I don't think hurts the fly's ability to fool fish. It might improve it.

Scuds are out in the water all year around, breeding, eating, or dashing about on errands. Trout turn to them at the odd times when no other food forms are active and available, simply because scuds are always active and available.

Periphyton pastures are the feeding grounds that attract scuds. You will find them browsing on rocks in water at the edges, just inches deep. Trout find them there, too, sometimes nosing in close to shore under the cover of darkness. More often, scuds are found burrowing deep into weed beds. Trout hang around the edges of the weeds, waiting to snipe at any that bumble out. Sometimes trout poke right into the beds, flushing scuds like quail and gunning them down on the wing.

If you hold a scud in your hand, it will be curled into half a ball, its swimmer legs tucked in. But observe them in the water sometime: They swim straight as sticks, almost always on their backs, swimmer legs awhir above them. That is why the best imitations are tied straight, not curved.

Scuds seem relatively directionless when they swim, just going until they get reattached to something or until their trajectories take them into danger, which they are helpless to dodge. When fishing scud dressings the best retrieve is fairly slow. It is also somewhat erratic. A hand-twist is usually best, but it should often be interspersed with a strip or two, representing a sudden burst of speed, and some twitching with the rod tip, indicating indecision.

The flies should always be weighted at least lightly because you'll always want to fish them down a bit. But you'll usually want to regulate the depth at which you fish them by selection of the correct sink rate line. The countdown method is especially effective with scuds. Get the fly down to where you want it. Then fish it level along the edges, or just over the top, of any weed beds that you can plumb down below.

Trout will intercept the fly subtly. You'll have to be wary for signs of the take.

CRAYFISH

At least one mountain lake I fish has an enormous population of crayfish. It has no inlet or outlet streams, and therefore no natural spawning. Two to three thousand trout are planted in it each spring as "catchables," 8 inches long. These grow and get caught throughout a summer of heavy pesterment by worm dunkers. As fall approaches, their numbers have dwindled to a few hundred. But these few have put up substantial growth and have gotten narrowly selective in self-defense. Bobber watchers can't catch them anymore.

Sometime in late summer most of the remaining trout reach a size where their mouths can encompass small crayfish. Then they suddenly balloon. By the end of the season some of them look like blimps, with tiny heads and tails and thick bodies in between.

The few that hold over until spring have dined all winter on the vast supply of crayfish. They've put on about a pound. The rare two- and three-year holdovers are 16 to 18 inches long and in fall weigh a couple of pounds or more, which is not large by all standards. But it is large for a small lake with no natural spawning.

I've never bothered to tie an exact imitation of the crayfish in this lake–for a simple reason. Its trout seem eager for Woolly Buggers, and a Woolly Bugger tossed to the shoreline and stripped

Although there are much more accurate imitations of crayfish, something like the Woolly Bugger does a better job of capturing the movement of the natural in the water. *Jim Schollmeyer*

out looks a lot like a crayfish dashing away from shore with a trout on its tail. I should say on its claws.

Crayfish swim with their tails. They point them where they want to go, then flip them rapidly, which races them backward through the water. Their claws trail behind them. With things moving so fast, these claws look a little like the extended tail of a Woolly Bugger. Although there are dozens of perfect patterns that look more like crayfish than crayfish do, I prefer to catch the action of the natural rather than its exact form.

Brown Woolly Bugger

Hook: 3X long #6 to #12

Thread: Brown

Weight: 12 to 15 turns lead wire

Tail: Brown marabou

Body: Brown chenille

Hackle: Furnace, palmered

An Olive Woolly Bugger also works. Many crayfish come in an olive shade with reddish brown mixed in. Others are almost bright red, but I haven't thought to try a red Woolly Bugger yet. It might do some damage. It also might turn the trout away. I'll try it. You try it, too.

The fast-stripping retrieve works best when fishing a streamer as a crayfish imitation. It also allows you to cover lots of water. When fish are scattered, it's a great way to explore for them. I usually do it in relation to the shoreline, flipping my tube or rowing my boat a cast out from the bank, shooting the fly in against it, letting it sink a little on a wet-tip line, then stripping it out.

This method takes a surprising number of trout for me. I haven't done enough interviews to know how many of them mistake the galloping Woolly Bugger for a crayfish.

CRESS BUGS

I have collected cress bugs in certain ponds but have yet to find them in a stillwater in sufficient numbers and the kind of availability that make them important to the trout fisherman. They are more important in spring creeks.

However, you will collect them in your wanderings, and it's wise to be familiar with them. An imitation will take fish, too, since trout might take it for a cress bug as well as any of a half dozen other creatures.

Cress bugs look a lot like scuds. But their aspect is flattened across the back, and their myriad legs are designed for walking rather than swimming. They look almost exactly like terrestrial sow bugs, also called pill bugs, which I hope we've all seen. They're about the same size, and their imitations should be tied on #14 and #16 hooks.

How's that for a simple dressing? In truth, you could just as well use a Gray Nymph or Gray Woolly Worm to accomplish the

---

Cress Bug

Hook: Standard or 1X long #14 to #16
Thread: Gray
Weight: 8 to 12 turns fine lead wire
Body: Muskrat fur dubbed loosely

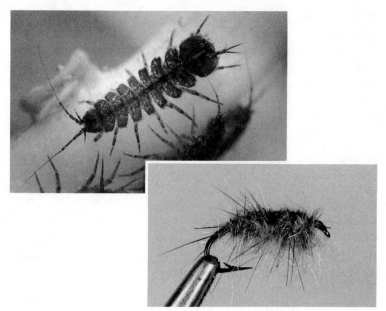

The natural cress bug is a hiker, not a swimmer. Its simple imitation should be fished at a creep, right along the bottom or near weed beds.
Jim Schollmeyer

same purpose. But this unadorned pattern looks more like the natural.

Cress bugs are always associated with vegetation or with the bottom. I've collected most specimens from leaf packs and silty detritus in dark waters that are already tragically eutrophic, in most cases beyond the point where they produce good trout fishing. That is why I've never found need to imitate them.

If you find fish feeding on them, your presentation should be near weed beds or close to the bottom, and it should be so slow it nearly bores you.

22

Leeches

Leeches are very important to the person who fishes stillwaters. The more I fish, the more I recognize that importance. They are not seen with great regularity in trout stomach samples, which means they are not getting eaten all of the time. But when a trout gets a chance, it loves to whack a leech. To a trout they're such a satisfying bite.

The right dressing, which recalls a leech to the trout, seems to elicit a response even when leeches aren't out and active. It seems that when an insect is out of momentary abundance, it is also out of the minds of fish, and its imitation is less likely to fool them. Leeches must stick in the memory longer than aquatic insects. Leech imitations fool them almost all of the time.

Leeches look like night crawlers that have been run over by trucks. They are flattened. They have suckers at both ends. The one at the stern is used for attachment, the one at the bow for both attachment and the ingestion of prey. Not all leeches are blood-suckers. Most of their diet consists of aquatic insects and whatever decaying life they can find.

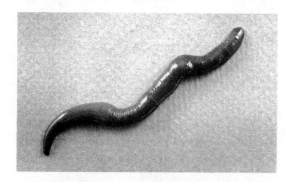

Natural leeches look a lot like night crawlers, but they're able to swim with an undulating motion. The best imitations such as the Woolly Bugger (left) and Mohair Leech capture the shape of the natural as well as its movement. *Jim Schollmeyer*

If you've never seen a leech, crack an egg into the shoreline shallows of a lake or pond sometime, just after dark. If they're around, they'll come galloping. My dad and I camped a few days on a little lake this summer. The folks there before us had cleaned fish right where we beached our boats. The fish guts were a windfall for leeches. Whenever we launched to go fishing, a herd of them got exposed by the sudden departure of the shelter they were hiding beneath. They were a dark olive that appeared almost black. They made it easy to decide to fish a Black Woolly Bugger.

Leeches average about two to three inches long. I've seen them much smaller, half an inch to an inch and a half long, and trout were feeding on them greedily. I've also seen them so large that they make me take a step backward in fear. They grow up to four and five inches long, and get fat from feasting.

Steve Raymond, in his classic stillwater study, *Kamloops*, noted that the largest specimens are rarely found in trout. He didn't know the reason. I don't know the reason. But my findings agree with his. Most of the leeches I've found in stillwater trout stomachs have been two to three inches long.

Most have been black, olive, or reddish brown. But leeches come in tan, too, with pretty black spots, and brown, and probably a lot of other colors that trout have seen but I have not.

Because they are so important, I'd like to suggest a couple of pattern styles for leeches. They're both standards, and both are easy to tie.

Woolly Bugger

Hook: 3X long #4 to #12

Thread: Olive, black, or brown

Weight: 10 to 15 turns lead wire

Tail: Olive, black, or brown marabou

Body: Olive, black, or brown chenille

Hackle: Black or brown, palmered

The standard olive dressing normally owns a brown hackle. For some reason – I think because a black hackle was lying on the bench when I tied my first Olive Woolly Buggers – my favorite dressing turns out to have a dark olive tail and body, but a black hackle. It doesn't make sense, and it really doesn't catch any more trout than the same dressing with a brown hackle. But that's the way I fish it most often.

I've seen times when a switch from one color to another resulted in sudden cooperation from reluctant trout. Since I almost always start off with the olive color, the switch is almost always to black. I don't use brown so much, although I've seen enough rusty brown leeches to know I should. But the olive has some reasoning behind it: Lots of large insects, such as dragonfly and damselfly nymphs, are also olive.

I've had fair luck tossing leeches in #4 and #6. But most of the time I prefer fishing with lighter gear, and therefore am more comfortable fishing with those in #10 and #12.

Mohair Leech

Hook: 3X long #4 to #12

Thread: Olive, brown, or red

Weight: 10 to 15 turns lead wire

Tail: Short strip of olive, brown, or red mohair

Body: Olive, brown, or red mohair roughed up on its core thread, then wound and swept back

---

The red version becomes a Blood Leech, one of the most effective in waters with brown and reddish brown leeches. I've seen times when a switch to this color took fish while they turned up cold noses at olive and black.

Other dressing styles also do a fine job representing leeches. The key is to capture their swimming movement, which is a series of undulations anywhere from slow to hectic depending on the messages being received by the sensors of the blind leech.

I learned something about fishing leeches from Paul Bech last summer. Paul is a fisheries biologist in British Columbia. His job, essentially, is to catch steelhead for the wild stock used in hatchery propagation. He uses sport gear, although to his shame not always fly gear, on his job. But Paul is a fellow who knows a bit about fish and a lot about trout. He fly-fishes when it's for recreation.

"When a trout takes a natural leech," Paul told me, "it overtakes the leech from behind, opens its mouth to flare its gills, and the leech is inhaled in the rush of water." It makes sense. But there is a problem.

"Most of the time a trout takes a leech from behind. But when a trout sneaks up behind a leech imitation and flares its gills, nothing happens: The fly is tethered to the leader." This must surprise the trout and cause it to frown. "Lots of times all you feel is a pluck. The standard response is to drop your rod, give the fly some slack, and hope the trout comes back and inhales it."

I used Paul's method on subsequent days and discovered he was exactly right. When fishing a leech I tried to develop the same response to a lake take that one must use when fishing for summer steelhead: Let everything go. It's difficult, but it's worth it. Whenever I felt a take, I would quell my urge to raise the rod and set the hook.

Most of the time when I lifted it again, a Kamloops rainbow would squirt into the air, the leech pattern in its jaw.

Leeches undulate along at all depths, but most of the time they are near vegetation or near the bottom. It's best to fish their imitations around some sort of structure: a weed bed, the shoreline, or in the shallows. Weight the flies enough to get them one or two feet down with a floating line. Beyond that, use a sinking line in the appropriate sink rate to get them down to the depth you want. Most of the time, for me, that means a wet-tip line. But there are lots of times when I fish leeches with the fast-sinking head in my shooting system.

I also tow leech dressings around lakes a lot, trolling and exploring in my float tube or pram. They are excellent for that. When I use them to explore this way, I usually have a midge dressing, a #12 or #14 TDC, on the leader two to three feet above the leech. Some folks say it makes the trout think something big is chasing something small. I don't know if trout think in those terms, but there is no reason to think they wouldn't. Greed is a good prod in the direction of survival.

I know that trout get greedy for leech patterns.

CONCLUSION

Let Lakes Come to You

It is customary to apologize for lakes. It goes like this: They are really challenging to fish once you learn them; you can catch bigger trout in lakes than you can in streams; not as many people like fishing lakes, so you can have them to yourselves. All of this is true some of the time, and some of the time it's not. But it doesn't matter. Fishing in lakes doesn't need any defense.

It's fun.

But it's best if you let the fun come to you.

Most people who would fish a stream for five or six hours in a day, during the period when insects and trout are most active, go out to a lake and hammer away at it from dawn to dusk. That's exhausting, which isn't what fishing should be. Fly-fishing is a sport. In at least some senses it's a relaxing one, although I'm not of the opinion that fly fishermen are as laid back as we'd like others to think we are.

Lakes are like streams: They have periods when things are going on, and they have periods when things are not going on. One of the secrets to fishing them successfully is learning when the periods of activity happen, and fishing intently then. Another of the secrets to successful stillwater fishing is to take it easy when activity is absent. Explore a little. Troll a fly. Paddle to shore and nose around the lake's environment. Poke your nose into what's going on in a shallow weed bed. Capture some insects or other aquatic creatures, then turn them loose and see how they swim.

Read a book.

Do something that increases the fun you have while on a lake or pond. And at the same time, try to increase your knowledge about the life of the stillwater. Then you'll begin to know when the fishing is going to get good.

And you'll have a lot more fun fishing when it is.

Bibliography

Borger, Gary A. *Nymphing*. Harrisburg: Stackpole Books, 1979.
———. *Naturals*. Harrisburg: Stackpole Books, 1980.
Cordes, Ron, and Randall Kaufmann. *Lake Fishing with a Fly*. Portland: Frank Amato Publications, 1984.
Curtis, Brian. *The Life Story of the Fish*. New York: Dover, 1949.
Hafele, Rick, and Dave Hughes. *The Complete Book of Western Hatches*. Portland: Frank Amato Publications, 1981.
Hafele, Rick, and Scott Roederer. *Aquatic Insects and Their Imitations*. Boulder: Johnson Books, 1987.
Hughes, Dave. *American Fly Tying Manual*. Portland: Frank Amato Publications, 1986.
———. *Western Streamside Guide*. Portland: Frank Amato Publications, 1987.
———. *Handbook of Hatches*. Harrisburg: Stackpole Books, 1987.
———. *Reading the Water*. Harrisburg: Stackpole Books, 1988.
———. *Tackle and Technique for Taking Trout*. Harrisburg: Stackpole Books, 1990.
———. *Tactics for Trout*. Harrisburg: Stackpole Books, 1990.
LaFontaine, Gary. *Caddisflies*. New York: Winchester Press/Nick Lyons Books, 1981.
McClane, A. J. *McClane's Standard Fishing Encyclopedia*. New York: Holt, Rinehart, and Winston, 1965.
Merwin, John, ed. *Stillwater Trout*. New York: Nick Lyons Books, 1980.
Meyer, Deke. *Float Tube Fly Fishing*. Portland: Frank Amato Publications, 1989.
Migel, J. Michael, ed. *The Masters on the Dry Fly*. New York: Nick Lyons Books, 1989.
Migel, J. Michael, and Leonard M. Wright, Jr., eds. *The Masters on the Nymph*. New York: Nick Lyons Books, 1979.

Morris, Skip. *The Custom Graphite Fly Rod.* New York: Nick Lyons Books, 1989.

Price, Taff. *Fly Patterns, an International Guide.* London: Ward Lock Ltd., 1986.

Raymond, Steve. *Kamloops.* Portland: Frank Amato Publications, 1980.

Roberts, Don. *Nymph Fishing Lakes.* Portland: Frank Amato Publications, 1978.

Rosborough, E. H. *Tying and Fishing the Fuzzy Nymphs,* 4th ed. Harrisburg: Stackpole Books, 1988.

Schwiebert, Ernest. *Trout.* New York: E. P. Dutton, 1978.

———. *Nymphs.* New York: Winchester Press, 1973.

Solomon, Larry, and Eric Leiser. *The Caddis and the Angler.* Harrisburg: Stackpole Books, 1977.

Stearns, Bob. *The Fisherman's Boating Book.* New York: Winchester Press/Nick Lyons Books, 1984.

Taylor, Marv. *Float-Tubes, Fly Rods and Other Essays.* Caldwell: Caxton Printers, 1979.

Usinger, Robert L., et al. *Aquatic Insects of California.* Berkeley: University of California Press, 1956.

Willers, W. B. *Trout Biology: An Angler's Guide.* New York: Lyons and Burford, 1991.

Index

Alderflies, 218–23

Back swimmers, 227–29
Boat bags, 63–64
Boats, bass, 79–80
  see also Canoes; Cartoppers; Float tubes;
    Prams

Caddisflies, 191–99
Caenis, 189–90
Callibaetis, 175–82
Canoes, 76–77, 78
Cartoppers, 76, 77–78
Clothing, 62–63, 64–65
Crayfish, 233–35
Cress bugs, 235–36

Damselflies, 212–17
Dragonflies, 208–12
Dry flies. See Flies, searching dry

Fishing strategy, 83–88
  see also specific fishing methods
Flies, nymph.
  fly selection for, 120–24
  methods for, 125–32
  tackle for, 124–25
  when to use, 117–18
  where to use, 118–20
Flies, searching dry.
  fly selection for, 94–95
  methods for, 95–97
  when to use, 91–93
  where to use, 93–94
Flies, streamer.
  casting pattern for, 151–52
  methods for, 146–51
  tackle for, 144–46
  when to use, 141–43
  where to use, 143–44
Flies, wet.
  fly selection for, 136–37
  methods for, 137–39
  tackle for, 137

when to use, 134–35
where to use, 135
Float tubes, 70–75
Fly boxes, 61–62
Fly patterns, selecting, 83–85, 103–5
  see also specific insects
Fly rods, 45–48

Hexagenia, 185–89
Hip boots, 67

Insects, aquatic.
  alderflies, 218–23
  back swimmers, 227–29
  caddisflies, 191–99
  damselflies, 212–17
  dragonflies, 208–12
  mayflies, 175–90
  midges, 200–207
  understanding behavior of, 105–6, 172–74
  water boatmen, 224–27

Lakes.
  chemical structure of, 29–32
  physical structure of, 20–25
  pollution and the chemistry of, 32
  temperature, stratification, and turnover
    of, 25–29
Leaders, 56–60
Leeches, 237–41
Lines, 48–56
  floating, 48–50
  floating/sinking system, 52–53
  full-sinking system, 53–55
  intermediate, 50–51
  shooting-head systems, 47–48, 55–56
  wet-tip, 50

Mayflies, 175–90
  caenis, 189–90
  callibaetis, 175–82
  hexagenia, 185–89
  siphlonurus, 183–85
Midges, 200–207

Nymph flies. *See* Flies, nymph

Prams, 75–76, 77–78

Reels, 60–61

Rods. *See* Fly rods

Scuds, 230–33
Sight fishing.
  approach for, 164–66
  detecting takes, 169–70
  presentation, 167–68
Siphlonurus, 183–85
Streamer flies. *See* Flies, streamer

Tackle.
  fly boxes, 61–62
  fly rods, 45–48
  leaders, 56–60
  lines, 48–56
  reels, 60–61

Trolling, 154–60
Trout.
  food, 13–14
  movements, 14–19
  need for oxygen and temperature, 7–10
  protection from predators, 3–7
  rising, 98–103, 110–13
  spawning, 10–13
  working a pod of, 107–10

Vegetation, aquatic.
  emergent, 34–35
  floating, 35–36
  planktonic growth, 37–38
  rooted, 33–34
  submerged, 36–37
  weed beds, 38–41

Waders, 68–70
Water boatmen, 224–27
Wet flies. *See* Flies, wet
Wind-drifting, 160–61